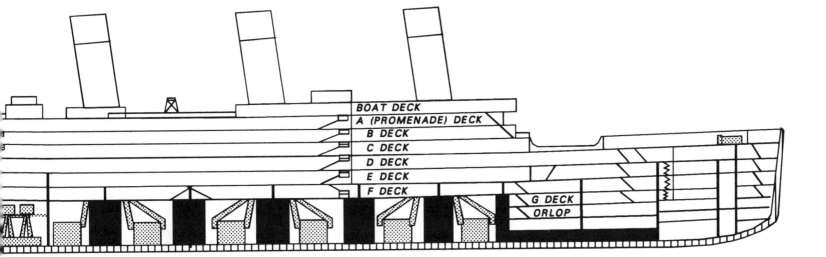

BOAT DECK
A (PROMENADE) DECK
B DECK
C DECK
D DECK
E DECK
F DECK
G DECK
ORLOP

TITANIC

AT

TWO A.M.

TITANIC

AT

TWO A.M.

PAUL J. QUINN

Fantail

Saco, Maine

Published January 1997
Second Printing June 1997
Third Printing October 1997

All paintings and diagrams are by Paul Quinn.
All black and white photographs are from the author's collection.

Library of Congress Catalog Card Number: 96-61655

ISBN   0-9655209-3-5

For Debi, who inspired me to paint and Elizabeth,
who helped make this book possible.

Printed and bound in the United States of America

Published by:

Fantail
P.O. Box 289
Saco, Maine 04072

CONTENTS

The Titanic beginning her maiden voyage.

Wednesday, April 10, 1912

Introduction

It was the middle of April in 1912 when a brand new ocean liner, the largest in the world, raced across the Atlantic on her way to New York City. She was the most lavish vessel on the high seas, complete with swimming pools, suites, restaurants, Turkish baths, squash courts, promenade walks, lounges, and even a sidewalk cafe of sorts. The ship was the Titanic. It took three years to build her, yet five days after she began her first trip she was two and a half miles beneath the surface of the ocean.

No other event in history played out so compellingly as the Titanic disaster - the latest in shipbuilding technology, loaded up with a cross section of society, thrown head on into a known danger despite repeated warnings. Once the damage had been done, 2,223 people had two hours and forty minutes to participate in a slowly unfolding disaster which would end with 706 survivors. A person lived or died that night based upon the choices they made after the collision.

The Titanic carried a variety of passengers, including those on business, people on vacation, and immigrants heading for America. Many were extremely wealthy with some being among the richest in the world. Others were very poor, searching for a better life once they arrived in New York. In addition to the 1,324 passengers, 899 members of the crew worked in a variety of functions on board. There were firemen at the boilers, bedroom stewards, dining room waiters, cooks, bellboys, engineers, officers, lookouts, barbers, a gymnasium instructor, musicians, radio operators, and more. Together, they represented the wealthy, the middle class, and the poor, complete with their personal lives in full session. Together, they all chose to sail on a ship that would go down in history.

In April of 1912, passenger traffic on the North Atlantic between Europe and America was heavy. Immigration to the United States and Canada was at an all time high as tens of thousands of people per month headed to America. The Industrial Age was in full swing, generating a class of business people traveling between the continents. It also created a large number of wealthy families who enjoyed vacationing in far away places. All of this created a boom in travel.

To many, crossing on the Atlantic Ocean was a necessary evil in order to get from one continent to the other. The prospect of spending a week on a ship as it rolled with the waves, while berthed in a tiny cabin, was not something everyone welcomed. A number of people considered ocean travel dangerous and did not care for the general conditions on board and the accompanying seasickness during the passage. Many passengers, immigrants included, were willing to pay a premium to travel on a ship that was fast, large, and safe.

The business of transporting all of these passengers in the early 1900's was extremely competitive. The notable companies involved in the market at the time were White Star Line, Cunard Line, French Line, Hamburg-Amerika Line, and the North German Lloyd Line. The largest amount of traffic was going in and out of New York City, and it was on this route that the lines often placed their state of the art ships. In an attempt to capture the lion's share of the market, these ships were getting bigger and faster with each passing year. In 1907, the Cunard Line introduced the sister ships Lusitania and Mauretania. They were both 790 feet long, and with a service speed of 24 to 25 knots, they were the biggest and fastest liners afloat at the time. The French Line was launching the liner France into service in late

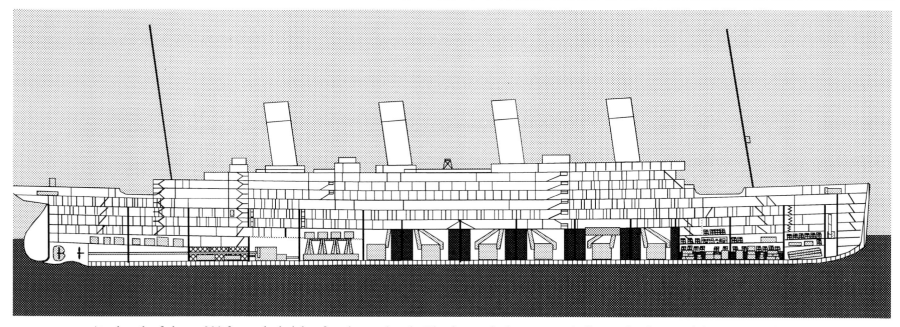

At a length of almost 900 feet and a height of twelve stories, the Titanic was the largest vessel afloat at the time - and the most luxurious.

April with a length of 713 feet and a speed of 24 knots. The North German Lloyd Line had their 707 foot long Kronprinzessin Cecilie in service since 1906 with a speed of 23 knots. Hamburg Amerika Line was constructing a trio of huge ships scheduled to go into service between 1913 and 1914, the first being the Imperator with a 919 foot length and a speed of 23 knots.

Bruce Ismay was the Managing Director of the White Star Line. After Cunard's Lusitania and Mauretania went into service, he immediately realized the need to update their flagship if they were to remain competitive. White Star Line was owned by J.P. Morgan's International Mercantile Marine, known as the I.M.M., and had the necessary financial resources for a market counterattack. Cunard's dazzling sister ships were the fastest afloat, White Star realized, but to achieve that speed the ships were restrained in size at 31,000 tons and were very expensive to operate because of the amount of coal they consumed. When White Star Line considered what type of ships they should build, they decided instead to focus on the other half of what passengers wanted - comfort.

Plans were put into place to build three sister ships which would be the largest in the world with names that would emphasize their size: Olympic, Titanic, and Gigantic. All would be approximately 45,000 tons, measure 882 feet long, and have a service speed of 21 to 22 knots. White Star figured passengers would forgo two or three knots of speed in exchange for larger accommodations and a steadier ship at sea. Construction began in 1908 and the Olympic was the first ship to be launched into service in June 1911 with much fanfare. By April 1912, the Titanic was ready. If everything continued according to plan, the three sister ships would soon be in full service and become the final word in luxury, safety, and reliability in ocean travel. Bruce Ismay and the White Star Line were well positioned for the North Atlantic passenger market and could not have been any prouder when the second of three ships was launched into service on April 10 for her maiden voyage.

One thing had changed by April 1912, however, since the trio of ships was first planned on the drawing boards. Originally, the slower 21 knot service speed was not supposed to matter since the three sister ships would stand out from their competition in size and luxury - and the Olympic and Titanic did for the time being. But larger liners were right around the corner. Hamburg-Amerika's 52,000 ton Imperator would go into service the following year with a service speed of 23 knots. When Cunard caught wind of the trio of ships White Star Line was constructing, they began construction of a 901 foot long 46,000 ton ship of their own to be called Aquitania, which also would have a service speed of 23 knots. White Star knew that

Titanic under construction in Ireland.

when the Titanic arrived in New York City on her maiden voyage, the press would focus on the new ship and, among other things, her speed would be reported in the papers. This press coverage would serve as the foundation for the public's first impression of the Titanic and it was a very important moment in the marketing of the new liner. Although it was impossible for the ship to set any kind of records, it was very desirable that the Titanic report a respectable crossing time. Accompanying the Titanic on her maiden voyage was Bruce Ismay. He wanted to see how the new ship did on her first trip out. He

was also taking note of her speed.

The Titanic departed from Southampton, England on Wednesday, April 10 at noon. Only minutes after setting off, the liner New York, tied up at dock, snapped her lines and drifted within feet of the Titanic, almost colliding with her stern. An accident was narrowly averted only through some quick maneuvering with the engines by Captain Smith, and the rush of tugboats to the New York's side. The incident was witnessed with great excitement by passengers as well as people on the docks who had come to see the Titanic off. After some delay, the Titanic resumed her voyage and headed for a passenger pick up at Cherbourg, France that afternoon. She then proceeded for Queenstown, Ireland for one last stop mid day Thursday to pick up more passengers. By two in the afternoon on Thursday, she was on her way again. As Ireland, and the world for that matter, saw the last of the Titanic, she was heading west, off into the impending sunset.

Throughout the voyage, the Titanic had good sailing weather. The sea was calm, the weather fair, and the passengers were impressed with the steadiness of the ship. There was one problem, however. When the coal was loaded onto the Titanic prior to she traveled 386 miles; Saturday, she did 519 miles and Sunday she traveled 546 miles. There was talk that the ship was going to do an all out run on Monday at maximum speed to see what the Titanic was capable of doing. Some hoped that the Titanic would surprise everyone and put in a showing as high as 23 knots. Bruce Ismay discussed the possibility of going full out and bringing the Titanic into New York Tuesday night instead of the scheduled Wednesday morning arrival time. It would make great news - Titanic arrives in New York on maiden voyage ahead of schedule. In the meantime, ships traveling in the opposite direction, coming from where the Titanic was heading, were sending wireless messages warning of ice.

As Sunday night rolled around, the Titanic lit more of her boilers and raced forward. The crew on watch were aware they were steaming into an ice region and all were put on alert to keep an eye out for it. Captain Smith was attending a dinner party in his honor at the A la Carte Restaurant most of the evening. Sometime after 9 P.M. he made an appearance on the bridge and advised Second Officer Lightoller to let him know if it looked at all doubtful. He then retired to his quarters. At 10 P.M. First Officer Murdoch took over the bridge. Lightoller

The First Class Reading and Writing Room. Many passengers wrote postcards and letters which were unloaded at the Titanic's last stop in Queenstown, Ireland. (Olympic)

departure, a fire ignited in the storage bunker and was still smoldering on the voyage. Attempts to put it out were unsuccessful and it continued its slow burn until finally on Saturday it was extinguished. Meanwhile, at 3 P.M. the same day, the Olympic departed from her New York berth bound for Southampton. There was some speculation that the two sister ships would pass each other on the Atlantic Monday afternoon.

The Titanic steadily increased her speed. From noon Thursday to noon Friday advised Murdoch they should be coming up on the ice region at any time and that the lookouts had been informed to keep a sharp eye out for ice.

Only forty minutes before the fateful collision, the ship Californian called the Titanic on the wireless to tell her that they were stopped in ice. The crew on the Californian could even see the Titanic approach on the horizon. But when the wireless operator on the Californian tapped in with the warning, the operator on the Titanic, who had just established contact with Cape Race, Newfoundland and was busy sending private messages, told the Californian "Shut up! Shut up! I am busy. I am working Cape Race." Listening in on his headphones a while longer, the Californian's operator finally put down his headset around 11:30 P.M.

At 11:40 on Sunday night, April 14th, the lookout high up on the Titanic's crow's nest spotted something dark ahead. There was no moon that night, the sea was black. Staring at the object for several seconds, it suddenly became clear what it was, and by the time the lookout telephoned the bridge with the word "Iceberg, right ahead!" the ship was coming straight up on it fast. First Officer Murdoch was in charge of the bridge

Captain Smith (right) rushed onto the bridge after the collision and asked First Officer Murdoch (left) what happened. Moments later the two gazed into the darkness for a glimpse of the iceberg.

at the time and quickly made the decision to reverse the engines and try to go around the left side of the iceberg. He ordered the helmsmen to "Hard a Starboard". It proved to be a fateful decision as the giant ship, racing forward, did not respond well to being thrown in reverse and having her rudder turned hard. The crew stood frozen as the Titanic seemed to ignore the turn of the wheel, and continued straight toward the iceberg. And then, just as it seemed certain that the ship was going to crash head on into the ice, the Titanic began to stubbornly turn

to port and the iceberg slid by along the right side of the ship.

The iceberg was enormous. It rose six stories out of the water and was at least a hundred feet wide. Down below, the steel plates cracked and buckled against the pressure of the ice as it rubbed along the starboard side of the ship. Passengers felt a slight shudder. Many were sleeping and the mild vibration was enough to wake some of them up; the rest never noticed and slept right through. As the iceberg drifted back into the blackness of the night, it left it's signature on the Titanic with a series of holes and cracks in her forward steel plates the length of a football field. In an instant the brand new Titanic had been dealt a death blow from the darkness of the Atlantic.

It was almost midnight when Captain Smith assessed the damage with the builder, Thomas Andrews and the owner, Bruce Ismay. Despite all of the watertight compartments designed to make the ship "practically unsinkable", in the words of the Shipbuilder Magazine, too many of them had been ruptured for the ship to stay afloat. The Titanic was going to sink. Once this point sank in and the shock passed, it was followed by another. There were 2,223 people on board and enough lifeboats to hold only

The Titanic's Officers

Captain Edward J. Smith. 62 years old. Was the Commodore of the White Star Line who transferred as Captain of the Olympic, the Titanic's twin sister ship. This was to be his final round trip voyage before retiring in England. He went down with the ship.

The Senior Officers

Chief Officer Henry Wilde. 38 years old. Transferred from the Olympic where he had been Chief Officer as well. Was to sail with Titanic just for the maiden voyage. Smith's late decision to transfer him from the Olympic resulted in Officers Murdoch and Lightoller getting bumped down one position. He went down with the ship.

First Officer William Murdoch. 38 years old. Transferred from the Olympic where he had been first officer. He was in charge of the bridge at the time of the collision. He went down with the ship.

Second Officer Charles Lightoller. 38 years old. Transferred from the Oceanic where he had been first officer. He was the only senior officer on the Titanic to survive.

The Junior Officers

Third Officer Herbert Pitman. 34 years old. Transferred from the Oceanic, where he had been second officer. He escaped in lifeboat 5.

Fourth Officer Joseph Boxhall. 28 years old. Transferred from the Arabic. He fired the distress rockets. He escaped in lifeboat 2.

Fifth Officer Harold Lowe. 28 years old. Was transferred from the Belgic where he had been third officer. He escaped in lifeboat 14.

Sixth Officer James Moody. 24 years old. Transferred from the Oceanic. Was on the bridge with Murdoch during the collision. Answered the phone from the crows nest to hear "Iceberg, right ahead." He was the only junior officer to not survive the disaster.

1,178. The largest ocean liner in the world was going to sink and there were not enough lifeboats for everyone.

Shortly after realizing the seriousness of the situation, Captain Smith made a decision which significantly added to the legend of this disaster. He clearly made up his mind that it was crucial there should be no panic. He advised his crew that the ship struck an iceberg, to wake the passengers and prepare the lifeboats for lowering. What he apparently did not do was make it clear to the officers responsible for evacuating the ship that the Titanic was actually going to sink. From the outset of the accident, the tone was set that women and children were to get into the boats as a precaution.

Passengers were aware that something was wrong when the engines stopped. Before Captain Smith had assessed the situation and issued orders, some came out of the cabins and assembled in the hallways to ask what was going on. Others went up on deck to look out into the night. It was a clear evening with intense starlight and no moon. The ocean was black and perfectly calm. It was very cold and most of the passengers who ventured out could not find anything wrong, so they went back inside to a warmer location like their cabins or the Reception Room down on D deck.

Eventually word came down of the captain's orders. Any remaining passengers who were still asleep were awakened by the stewards. There were no sirens or alarms. Simply a knock at the door with instructions by the cabin steward to put on a life jacket and proceed immediately to the boat deck - that is, if the person was a first or second class passenger. Many passengers did not even learn until they reached the boat deck that lifeboats were actually being lowered with passengers in them. The stewards explained it was simply a precaution and there was nothing serious to worry about. To the stewards, this official explanation was not a deception. As far as they were concerned, this was the truth. So the first and second class passengers straggled up to the boat deck. Some went up immediately while others took their time, going up as late as an hour after first being told to do so. Some dressed fully while others ascended the steps in just a bathrobe and slippers. Some went straight up to the boat deck, while others went to the lounges. At first, nobody told them where to go once they came up the stairs. Since there had been no lifeboat drill on the voyage, they assembled all over, including the lounges, the smoking rooms, the gymnasium, the Promenade Deck, and the boat deck.

In third class, passengers were told to put on their life belts and report up on deck. But they only made it to the foot of their main staircase on D deck before meeting crewmen who advised them to wait there until further direction.

One by one the boats were lowered. Because the tone was set that there was nothing to worry about, most of the earlier lifeboats lowered were not even half filled. One by one they dropped - all of them under capacity. It appears from testimony afterwards that a combination of three things occurred to worsen the number of people that would die. The first was that the passengers themselves did not see any point early on in climbing into a lifeboat that was literally dangling over the side of the Titanic, some seventy feet above the dark Atlantic in the middle of the cold night, when it was only a precaution. The second was a rule followed by the officers on the port side of the ship, particularly the second officer, Charles Lightoller. Rather than follow the instructions issued by the captain of "women and children first", Lightoller consistently followed the rule, women and children *only*. As a result, early on when there was trouble in filling up the boats with enough women and children, he would send the boats away half empty even if there were men willing to go. Finally, all of the officers were concerned about loading the boats up to their capacity for fear that they would break in two and spill the passengers into the water below. They were unaware that the lifeboats had been tested just before the voyage with a full compliment of people and passed. So they chose instead to reduce the maximum number of people to approximately half of what the boat could really carry. The officers originally planned to load more passengers into them once they were in the water from gangway doors closer to the water. This disastrous plan never succeeded. Crewmen sent down to open the doors never returned, and the boats, once lowered, disobeyed the orders and never came back alongside the ship. So for these three reasons, an already bad situation was made much worse and 400 more people died unnecessarily.

In 1912 the only radio that existed

The U.S. Senate Titanic Disaster Hearings

As the world reeled from the shock of the Titanic disaster, many quickly asked how such a horrible disaster could have happened. Before the rescue ship Carpathia even arrived in New York on the evening of Thursday, April 18, the United States Senate, lead by Senator William Alden Smith of Michigan, moved to begin formal proceedings into the causes of the Titanic disaster. While the Carpathia was still at sea with the survivors, the U.S. Senate passed the following resolution.

In the Senate of the United States
April 17, 1912.

Resolved, That the Committee on Commerce, or a subcommittee thereof, is hereby authorized and directed to investigate the causes leading to the wreck of the White Star liner Titanic, with its attendant loss of life so shocking to the civilized world.

Resolved further, That said, committee or a subcommittee thereof is hereby empowered to summon witnesses, send for persons and papers, to administer oaths, and to take such testimony as may be necessary to determine the responsibility therefor, with a view to such legislation as may be necessary to prevent, as far as possible, any repetition of such a disaster.

Resolved further, That the committee shall inquire particularly into the number of life boats, life rafts, and life preservers, and other equipment for the protection of the passengers and crew; the number of persons aboard the Titanic, whether passenger or crew, and whether adequate inspections were made of such vessel, in view of the large number of American passengers traveling over a route commonly regarded as dangerous from icebergs; and whether it is feasible for Congress to take steps looking to an international agreement to secure the protection of sea traffic, including regulation of the size of ships and designation of routes.

Resolved further, That in the report of said committee it shall recommend such legislation as it shall deem expedient; and the expenses incurred by this investigation shall be paid from the contingent fund of the Senate upon vouchers to be approved by the chairman of said committee.

These hearings began on Friday, April 19 at the Waldorf Astoria in New York City and ran through Saturday evening. They were then resumed on Monday in Washington D.C. and continued until May 18. During the course of these hearings, testimony was heard from 88 witnesses. The investigation culminated with a speech on the Senate floor on May 28, 1912.

Although numerous accounts have been furnished of the disaster by hundreds of survivors, the testimony put forth during the hearings deserves a special place when assessing historical accuracy. The accounts furnished are the only accounts provided under oath to the U.S. Government within *days* of the disaster - still fresh in the memories of those furnishing the information and without the elaboration and exaggeration frequently seen in many of the newspapers of the day. Many of the accounts furnished in this book are direct from the hearings.

was the Morse code system of communication. Words were transmitted one letter at a time through a series of radio signals made up of long and short buzzes. Just after midnight, Captain Smith issued instructions to the operator, Jack Phillips, to send out the call for assistance and advise that the Titanic was sinking. But again, fate was against the ship. Captain Smith soon learned from Phillips that every ship responding to their distress signal was too far to get to the Titanic in time.

At 12:45, the Captain issued orders to send up rockets to gain the attention of the mysterious ship seen on the horizon. This ship was the steamer Californian - the same ship that had watched the Titanic come up on the horizon and the same ship that had tried to warn the Titanic of the ice field. Now, the ship sat quietly in the distance. With her radio turned off, she was not responding to the Titanic's SOS signals. The wireless operator on the Californian had gone to bed.

Once the rockets were sent up into the air, there was an increased sense of urgency on the Titanic. If the lifeboats were being sent away just as a precautionary measure, then it seemed it was a rather serious precaution. From that point onward there was a growing interest by the passengers to climb into the boats. But much of the damage was done since, pathetically, many of the boats were already lowered with too many empty seats.

By 2:00 A.M., two lifeboats remained in the davits. Of the 1,600 people left on the Titanic, approximately 100 would survive. Individually, any of them could have saved themselves had they done something

Some passengers assembled in the first class Reception Room awaiting news on why the ship stopped. They were soon told to get their lifebelts on and go up to the boat deck. (Olympic)

different earlier in the evening. But now, time was running out and with each passing minute their fate was falling into the same hands that held the Titanic. This is the story of the final twenty minutes of the ship and the dark hours that followed her sinking.

The Ship On The Horizon - Part I

Was It The Steamer Californian?

One of the most interesting aspects of the Titanic disaster is the fact that, as the great liner sank, there was a ship on the horizon to the north that did not come to her rescue. This mysterious ship appeared to be heading toward the Titanic at one point, only to turn and head away to the west, leaving 1,500 people to freeze to death in the cold Atlantic. Who was this ship? The survivor's testimonies are riddled with inconsistencies but when all the evidence is fitted together, the likely answer is the obvious one - that the ship on the horizon was the cargo steamer Californian. This was the same conclusion reached after the U.S. Senate Hearings and the British Inquiry.

Even though the crew on the Californian had watched a ship on the horizon fire rockets, to his dying day Captain Stanley Lord of the Californian disputed that his ship was the one seen by the Titanic. He insisted he was too far away at the time. Witnesses on both the Titanic and Californian testified that the ship each of them saw in the distance was moving. The Californian was stopped in ice - and of course, the Titanic was not going anywhere at the time except toward the bottom of the ocean. By his own calculations based on the reported location of the Titanic, he was 20 miles away and it would have taken him "at the very least two hours" to reach the foundering liner. Since the first distress rockets were fired at 12:45 A.M. and the ship sank one hour and thirty-five minutes later, they would have been too late even if they had headed for the Titanic right away.

Sympathizers of Captain Lord's position suggest there was a mysterious third ship steaming in between the Titanic and Californian. As this mystery ship traveled by, they could see the Titanic to the south, and the Californian to the north. The theory holds that the Titanic and Californian were too far over the horizon to see each other, but that both could see this third ship in between. It is an inviting theory for sure. Although it is a great answer to several inconsistencies in accounts that evening, no ship in that area ever fit the bill as being the mystery ship.

There are accounts about the lights seen on the horizon, most of them brief. Many on the Titanic were preoccupied with activities on deck at the time and only glanced at the light on the horizon with the naked eye, battling deck lights in the process. Two people paid close attention to the ship on the horizon - Captain Smith and Fourth Officer Joseph Boxhall. Boxhall survived to testify at the Senate Inquiry and much weight should be placed on his observations since he was specifically tasked by Captain Smith to try to communicate with the ship. As a result, he spent considerable time studying it in the darkness of the bridge.

There are also eyewitness accounts from the crew of the Californian who also saw a ship in the distance. With one exception, these witnesses were officers who probably realized the implications of having watched a ship on the horizon fire eight rockets into the sky without going to their assistance. Second Officer Herbert Stone and Apprentice James Gibson were on watch and testified at the British Inquiry about the rockets they had seen.

Ernest Gill, on the other hand, was a seaman on the Californian with little to lose by speaking candidly about what happened on the night of April 14, 1912. Captain Lord later tried to discredit Gill by pointing out that he had been paid $500 for his story by a newspaper. But unlike the other officers on the Californian who were at risk of sharing responsibility for 1,500 deaths, Gill had no responsibility for the actions of the Californian that night, and was definitely in a better position to comment freely on events.

Boxhall and Gill's testimonies bear amazing consistencies to each other at a detailed level. Reviewed in sequence, they imply there was no ship between them. Instead they illustrate that the Titanic and Californian were watching each other with great interest the entire time.

The Californian arriving on the scene of the disaster Monday morning.

From the Californian

Ernest Gill: "It was very clear and I could see for a long distance. The ship's engines had been stopped since 10:30 and she was drifting amid floe ice. I looked over the rail on the starboard side and saw the lights of a very large steamer about 10 miles away. I could see her broadside lights. I watched her for fully a minute. They could not have helped but see her from the bridge and lookout. It was now 12 o'clock and I went to my cabin. I woke my mate, William Thomas. He heard the ice crunching alongside the ship and asked, 'Are we in the ice?' I replied, 'Yes'."

From the Titanic

Senator Fletcher: "What kind of steamer was that which you saw ... as to size and character?"

Joseph Boxhall: "That is hard to state, but the lights were on masts which were fairly close together - the masthead lights."

Fletcher: "What would that indicate?"

Boxhall: "That the masts were pretty close together. She might have been a four mast ship or might have been a three mast ship, but she certainly was not a two mast ship."

Fletcher: "You know it was a steamer and not a sailing vessel?"

Boxhall: "Oh yes; she was a steamer, carrying steaming lights - white lights."

Fletcher: "Was she a sailing vessel?"

Boxhall: "No, sir; a sailing vessel does not show steaming lights, or white lights."

In the above accounts, Gill describes the approach of a large steamer. The Titanic was a large steamer. Boxhall describes a steamer with three or four masts. The Californian had four masts.

From the Titanic

Boxhall: "At first I saw two masthead lights of a steamer, just slightly opened, and later she got closer to us, until eventually, I could see her side lights with my naked eye."

Fletcher: "Was she approaching you?"

Boxhall: "Evidently she was, because I was stopped."

Fletcher: "And how far away was she?"

Boxhall: "I considered she was about 5 miles away."

Fletcher: "In what direction?"

Boxhall: "She was headed toward us, meeting us."

Fletcher: "Was she a little toward your port bow?"

Boxhall: "Just about half a point off our port bow."

From the Californian

Ernest Gill: "I turned in but could not sleep. In half an hour I turned out, thinking to smoke a cigarette. Because of the cargo I could not smoke 'tween decks, so I went on deck again. I had been on deck about 10 minutes when I saw a white rocket about 10 miles away on the starboard side."

Fletcher: "In what direction were the rockets from the Californian when you first saw them?"

Gill: "On the starboard side, forward."

Boxhall saw the masthead lights of the other ship "just slightly opened", indicating that the bow of the other ship was pointed in the direction of the Titanic - but not directly at her. Gill relates that he saw the other ship off the starboard bow, indicating that the Californian was pointed in the direction of the distant light - but not directly at it.

From the Titanic

Boxhall: *"I had been firing off rockets before I saw her side lights. I fired off the rockets and then she got so close I could see her side lights and starboard light."*

From the Californian

Fletcher: *"Did you observe the rockets go up in the direction this ship was as you first saw her, from where the Californian was?"*
Gill: *"It was more abeam, sir; more broadside of the ship."*

Boxhall stated the other ship, after pointing at the Titanic, turned broadside. Gill's account shows that first the Californian was aimed in the general direction of the other ship, but then turned "more broadside". Based on Gill's testimony, the Californian was drifting in a counterclockwise motion with her bow first aimed at the distant ship and then her side.

It would stand to reason, the Californian would eventually turn her stern to the distant light as she continued her counterclockwise drift.

From the Titanic

Boxhall: *"I saw that light, saw all the lights, of course, before I got into the boat, and just before I got into the boat she seemed as if she had turned around. I saw just one single bright light then, which I took to be her stern light."*

When the Californian's stern drifted around to the Titanic's direction, those on the Titanic mistook the ship as steaming away - when in fact it was still stationary.

In addition to the tight fit of how these ships appeared to move in relation to each other, there are accounts of the two officers on watch on the Californian at the time - Stone and Gibson. They were on the bridge observing the horizon light with great interest through binoculars. It came to light at the British Inquiry that the following observations were made that night as the two watched the distant ship fire rockets into the air.

From the Californian

Herbert Stone: *"A ship is not going to fire rockets at sea for nothing. Have a look at her now, Gibson. She seems to look queer now."*
James Gibson: *"She looks rather to have a big side out of the water."*

As one can see, there is significant evidence to indicate the Californian was indeed the ship on the horizon. The greatest evidence is that the Californian's own crew watched eight rockets fired into the air right over the distant light. How could this have been any other ship but the Titanic?

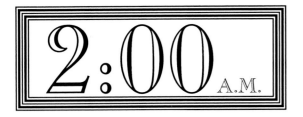

Since the collision, the Titanic sank at such a slow pace that most passengers still on board at 2:00 A.M. scarcely noted any deterioration in the ship's condition from one minute to the next. It had been two hours and twenty minutes since the Titanic struck the iceberg. The ship obviously was damaged as evidenced by the tilt of her decks, but many still did not think the situation was dangerous. The Titanic supposedly had "watertight" compartments. It was widely believed that the watertight bulkheads would keep the ship afloat. Many passengers still on board reasoned that when the damaged areas of the ship filled with water, the watertight compartments would eventually stop the rest of the ship from flooding. They believed the Titanic would settle in the water until a certain point, and then remain afloat in that position until help arrived.

By now, just 600 people had evacuated the ship with only twenty minutes left before the Titanic foundered. They rowed away in lifeboats and watched the gigantic ocean liner settling down by the head. Many had no idea how bad off the Titanic was until they saw her from the water. With her stern rising and the bow almost completely submerged, the extent of the ship's sinking was a shock.

The locations of those remaining on board were polarized at 2:00 A.M., to a large extent, between those assembled near the last lifeboats being lowered at the forward end of the boat deck and those third class passengers down on the steerage decks at the stern. There were some passengers and crew between, but most were at these two locations. At the forward end of the boat deck, two lifeboats remained. Both of them were "collapsibles" consisting of canvas sides that folded up into place, and identified by the letters "C" and "D". C was on the starboard side and D on the port. Both were stored underneath the forward lifeboats. Now, with only twenty minutes left, a large group of people assembled near them, mostly first and second class men, in hopes of getting a seat.

Scattered about other areas of the ship were crew who no longer knew what to do with themselves. They were a mixed group - firemen from the boiler rooms, stewards from the cabin areas, bellboys, cooks, and a few engineers. Some were near the forward lifeboats, but many simply stood around and waited on time. Frankie Goldsmith recalled seeing some of them.

Frankie Goldsmith: "My little boy's eyes recall looking into windows and open spaces of the two decks we were being lowered past ... I saw early teenage boys who were employed aboard the ship in several capacities. They, believe it or not, were playing games and some were smoking cigarettes, an action that was normally denied them."

A number of men were gathered in the first class Smoking Room, biding their time. Steeped in Edwardian leather chairs,

The First Class Smoking Room

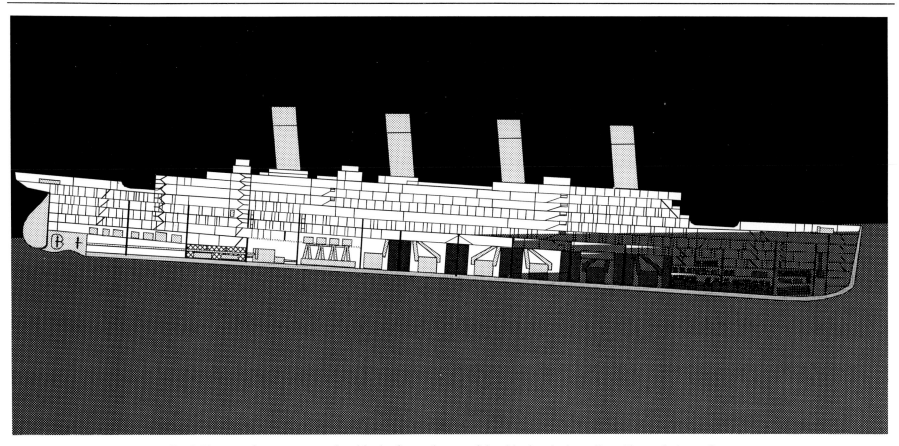

By 2:00 so much water accumulated in the forward areas of the ship that the bow dipped beneath the surface.

stained glass windows, and mother of pearl inlaid paneling, the room was a cozy harbor from the crowds and temperature. It was cold outside and for the men who were unattached or had already seen their wives and families off into lifeboats, this was a good place to wait out whatever was going to happen. They knew the Titanic represented the latest in technology and that her watertight bulkheads would keep the ship afloat. And if some of the rumors were true, and the ship was actually going to sink, well, the watertight compartments would keep the ship afloat long enough for help to arrive. They heard through the grapevine that the wireless room was sending out the call for assistance. So while all these events worked themselves out, they prided themselves on their cool headedness and cleverness to remain indoors in cozy comfort while the rest either bobbed about in lifeboats in the Atlantic, or stood outside in the cold on the open decks. The lights were burning bright, the drinks were still flowing, and even though the slant of the linoleum floor had definitely worsened, the ship still seemed solid. Several were even engaged in a card game.

The second class public rooms were generally deserted most of the evening. But now, some passengers and crew at the forward end of the boat deck were abandoning hope of getting a seat in the last two lifeboats and heading for the stern. On their way, they wandered by the second class smoking room at the very rear of B deck, and the lounge on C. Located near the stern on these higher decks, they offered a warm and comfortable space to wait out events. Only the third class open well and poop decks were further back and those areas were very crowded with steerage passengers, many of whom did not speak English.

As 2:00 A.M. rolled around, the gates holding back the remaining steerage passengers were opened. Third class passengers had been kept back toward the stern of the ship on the lower C and D decks throughout most of the evening. Many of them did not realize the severity of the situation and further, did not even realize that they were being discriminated against. It was

the age of classes, and everyone had their place. Many of these passengers knew their so-called places in life and did not question or understand the treatment they received that night. Even those that survived did not seem to question why they had been forced to remain in their area while the lifeboats in the first and second class areas were lowered away - predominantly with first and second class passengers.

Olaus Abelseth was one of these passengers. Being a male third class passenger, he was in the most discriminated category. He did not get off the ship in a lifeboat and was lucky to have survived. Most third class men perished that night. At the Senate Inquiry, he described what he saw in the third class area at the stern.

Olaus Abelseth: "There were a lot of steerage people there that were getting on one of those cranes that they had on deck, that they used to lift things with. These steerage passengers were crawling along on this, over the railing, and away up to the boat deck. A lot of them were doing that."
Senator Smith: "They could not get up there in any other way?"
Abelseth: "This gate was shut."
Smith: "Was it locked?"

Abelseth: "I do not know whether it was locked, but it was shut so that they could not go that way. A while later these girls were standing there, and one of the officers came and hollered for all of the ladies to come up on the boat deck. The gate was opened and these two girls went up."

Later in the questioning ...

Smith: "I want to direct your attention again to the steerage. Do you think the passengers in the steerage and in the bow of the boat had an opportunity to get out and up on the decks, or were they held back?"
Abelseth: "Yes, I think they had an opportunity to get up."
Smith: "There were no gates or doors locked, or anything that kept them down?"
Abelseth: "No, sir. Not that I could see."
Smith: "You said that a number of them climbed up on these cranes?"
Abelseth: "That was on the top, on the deck, after they got on the deck. That was in order to get up on this boat deck."
Smith: "Onto the top deck?"
Abelseth: "Onto the top deck; yes. But down where we were, in the rooms, I do not think there was anybody that held anybody back."
Smith: "You were not under any restraint?"

You were permitted to go aboard the boats the same as other passengers?"
Abelseth: "Yes, sir."

Abelseth's testimony is extraordinary in illustrating the attitudes and expectations of many in the "lower" class during this age. Even though he specifically describes how people had to climb cranes in order to get up to the boat decks, and describes how gates were shut to prevent people from going up to the higher decks, and relates how the crew eventually called for ladies only to go up, and even though he is then specifically prompted by Senator Smith to express whether he thinks the third class passengers were kept back, Olaus Abelseth states he does not think so.

Accurate information was probably scarce in third class. Because the lifeboats were located in the first and second class areas, they were not directly exposed to the drama of the evacuation. Instead, they had to rely heavily on what the Titanic's crew were telling them.

Olaus Abelseth: "We all went up on deck and stayed there. We walked over to the port side of the ship and there were five of us standing, looking, and we thought we saw a light. We were then on the port side there, and we looked out at this light. I said to my brother-in-law: 'I can see it plain, now. It must be a light'. It did not seem to be so very far. I thought I could see this mast light, the front mast light. A little while later there was one of the officers who came and said to be quiet, that there was a ship coming."

From their vantage point leaning over the railing of well deck at the stern, only some could see lifeboats being lowered toward the front of the ship. But there was no way from down on the well and poop decks to tell how many lifeboats were left. They had no idea there were too few lifeboats for all of the passengers. As far as they knew, the Titanic's crew were properly looking out for them and were simply maintaining order by making them wait until the time was right to bring them up. When women were allowed up to the boat decks, many chose not to go because they were with their families. They had no intention of leaving their husbands and their sons, particularly if they thought that in a while everyone would be allowed up to the lifeboats anyway.

There were also third class passengers, however, who realized the danger early on. These passengers took control of their situations and set off for the lifeboats early in assorted ways. First, there were the women who took advantage of the opportunity to go up to the boat deck the moment the crew allowed ladies to go. Then there were the men who climbed the cranes to the higher decks. Others set off inside the ship and found ways up to the higher decks. These passengers reached the boat deck, and for the women in particular, found a seat in a lifeboat. Many of these third class passengers were unattached and were able to set off independently in their quest for the lifeboats.

It is probably true that a number of third class passengers refused to go up to the boat deck when offered the chance, but the circumstances surrounding their decision should be taken into account. Many were with families traveling to America to start a new life. Some did not speak English and were not fully aware of what exactly was happening. They did not want to separate from each other at such an upsetting time. In the first and second class, the entire family was allowed to go up to the edge of the lifeboat. There, the man could at least see his wife into the boat and his wife could clearly see that it was the direction of the officers - women and children first. But in third class, when the word came down that women could go up to the boat deck, the situation was more anxious. Standing in the middle of a crowd in a shadowy light on a tilting ship with the lifeboats nowhere in sight and several decks above, it would have been very difficult for a family or a group traveling together to split up. So they stayed together at the stern.

Finally, the crew who were relentlessly guarding the steps up to the higher decks let all steerage passengers, not just women and children, up from the open well on C deck to the second class promenade areas on B deck. From that point onward they were left on their own to figure out how to get up to the boat deck.

So at 2:00 A.M., there remained mostly first and second class men at the very forward end of the boat deck still hoping to get a seat on the last lifeboat hanging in the davits. At the same time, toward the stern, there was a sudden release of large numbers of passengers who began their journey through the various hallways and up the deck ladders to get to the boats. Along the way, they would meet various people heading in the opposite direction. These people, mostly men and a handful of women who refused to be separated from their husbands, decided there was no further point in lingering about

Lifeboat 4 rows alongside the ship in search of an open gangway door.

on the boat deck and headed for higher ground.

Down in the water lifeboat number 4 was rowing along the port side of the ship. They were lowered five to ten minutes before 2:00 A.M. and experienced great difficulty getting the ropes and tackle free from the boat. It was just around 2:00 A.M. when they succeeded in getting free of the lines and underway.

Emily Ryerson: "Someone shouted something about a gangway, and no one seemed to know what to do. Barrels and chairs were being thrown overboard."

Mrs. Stephenson: "When we finally were ready to move the order was called from the deck to go to the stern hatch and take off some men. There was no hatch open and we could see no men, but our crew obeyed orders, much to our alarm, for they were throwing wreckage over and we could hear a cracking noise resembling china breaking. We implored the men to pull away from the ship, but they refused, and we pulled three men into the boat who had dropped off the ship and were swimming towards us. One man was drunk and had a bottle of brandy in his pocket which the quartermaster promptly threw overboard and the drunken man was thrown into the bottom of the boat and a blanket thrown over him."

Jack Thayer, the son of one of the women in lifeboat 4, may have bumped into the same man a few minutes earlier on deck.

Jack Thayer: "Our own situation was too pressing, the scene too kaleidoscopic for me to retain any detailed picture of individual behavior. I did see one man come through the door out onto the deck with a full bottle of Gordon Gin. He put it to his mouth and practically drained it. If ever I get out of this alive, I thought, there is one man I will never see again. He apparently fought his way into one of the last two boats, for he was one of the first men I recognized upon reaching the deck of the S.S. Carpathia."

Rowing alongside the ship toward the stern in search of some particular gangway door that was supposed to be open, the Titanic must have been terrifying. Every once in a while they would see a porthole open with the sea pouring into the cabin. Some of these cabins were lit inside and the lifeboat occupants could see the water swirling in and about the furniture. In the

While lifeboat 4 rowed along just outside the dining room windows, the sound of breaking china could be heard from somewhere within.

meantime, looming over them was the ship, lights still burning bright with row after row of portholes, all heading down at an angle into the water. Chairs were being randomly tossed over the side and some of them were splashing into the sea too close for comfort. They must have been very preoccupied with the thought of one of those chairs - or even a person - crashing down right into their boat.

Meanwhile, off on the horizon just to the left of where the Titanic's bow was pointing, a single bright light of the distant steamer Californian could still be seen. Those on the Titanic of course, did not know the identity of the vessel. At one point, this mysterious ship appeared to be heading for the Titanic, and then within the last hour or

When Did Collapsible C Leave The Ship?

Collapsible C was the last lifeboat to leave the starboard side of the Titanic and one of the more famous boats because it carried one of the Titanic's owners, Bruce Ismay, on board. Most estimates of when the lifeboat departed vary between 1:30 and 1:40 A.M.. Two particular accounts, George Rowe's and Hugh Woolner's, indicate that it was instead much later and only minutes before collapsible D left around 2:05 to 2:10 A.M..

Rowe observes that the C deck well was submerged when they reached the water on the starboard side. By that time, the Titanic was leaning significantly to port. If C deck was submerged on the starboard side then the water must have been at least as high as B deck on the port side. Collapsible D was lowered on the port side when the water was flowing over the A deck railing. It would not have taken very long for the water to climb

WHERE COLLAPSIBLE C WAS LOWERED

from B deck to the A deck railing.

Next comes Woolner's account. After collapsible C was loaded, they went down to A deck. They found no one on the starboard side and then crossed over to the port side. From there, they went through the front doors of the enclosed promenade and met collapsible D on its way down to the water.

All of this happened in sequence and could not have taken that much time. When Woolner described an event surrounding the lowering of collapsible D, he was questioned about the time.

Senator Smith: "How long was that after the collapsible lifeboat (C) ... was lowered?"
Woolner: "Oh, quite a few minutes; a very few minutes."

In addition to Rowe and Woolner's accounts, Chief Officer Wilde appeared at collapsible D just before it was lowered. It makes perfect sense that once collapsible C was lowered he would have proceeded immediately to D, the last remaining lifeboat.

All of this points to the conclusion that collapsible C, with Ismay in it, left very close to the time collapsible D was lowered - only minutes before the final plunge.

so, it seemed to turn. Now it appeared to be steaming away. Many could not believe it and some concluded the ship must be a star, or several stars that had mislead everyone on board. Surely, no ship would turn her back on the sinking Titanic in the icy Atlantic at this time of night. As the final minutes ticked away on the sinking ship, the distant light seemed to sit on the horizon like some disinterested cat on a window sill.

But the light was not a star. With her radio turned off, the two officers on the Californian's bridge continued to watch the Titanic right up to the end. Several times that night, two of the crew on watch informed their captain, who was lying down below deck, about a ship that was firing rockets. He advised them to try and signal the other ship with the Morse lamp. In parallel, Captain Smith advised Fourth Officer Boxhall to try and Morse the mystery ship as well. Each in turn, at one time or another, thought they could actually see some kind of response. But the light was so faint that it could not be made out. Unfortunately, the two ships watched each other as the Titanic sank lower and lower. As the bow of the Titanic dipped under, the Californian believed they were watching the distant ship steam away. This effect worked the same way on the Titanic.

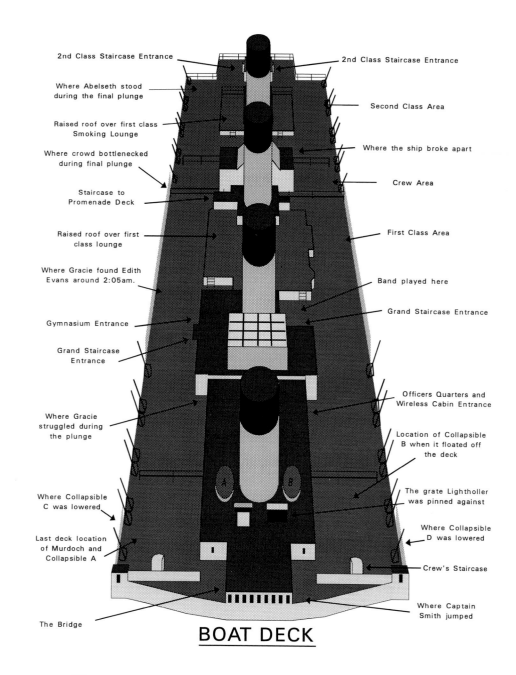

2nd Class Staircase Entrance

Where Abelseth stood during the final plunge

Raised roof over first class Smoking Lounge

Where crowd bottlenecked during final plunge

Staircase to Promenade Deck

Raised roof over first class lounge

Where Gracie found Edith Evans around 2:05am.

Gymnasium Entrance

Grand Staircase Entrance

Where Gracie struggled during the plunge

Where Collapsible C was lowered

Last deck location of Murdoch and Collapsible A

The Bridge

2nd Class Staircase Entrance

Second Class Area

Where the ship broke apart

Crew Area

First Class Area

Band played here

Grand Staircase Entrance

Officers Quarters and Wireless Cabin Entrance

Location of Collapsible B when it floated off the deck

The grate Lightoller was pinned against

Where Collapsible D was lowered

Crew's Staircase

Where Captain Smith jumped

BOAT DECK

As she sank closer to the surface, the distant light of the steamer became harder to see, until many could not see it anymore.

At 2:00 A.M., collapsible D on the port side was ready for loading. It was stored underneath lifeboat 2 and when that boat had been launched about 15 minutes earlier, D was waiting right there. Now the canvas sides were pulled up and locked into place and the boat was swung out over the railing along the side of the ship. There it was. The last lifeboat that would be launched from the ship with 1,600 people still on board!

Collapsible D could have been loaded efficiently but, like most of the lifeboats that night, it was not. Just as this boat was prepared for loading, an officer shouted: "All passengers to the starboard side!" The timing of this order is unfortunate because it created confusion at a period when there was no time to spare. The result was that when a call went out for women and children to climb into the lifeboat, for a few moments, virtually no one was there!

In the meantime, collapsible C on the starboard side was already loaded and about to be lowered under Chief Officer Wilde and First Officer Murdoch's supervision. Women trickled up to the boat at a painstakingly slow pace. A final call went out for any more ladies or children. The last to climb aboard were from third class, arriving from the stern in small groups.

Suddenly, passengers who were following orders started arriving in large numbers from the other side of the ship - just in time to crowd Murdoch's efforts to finish loading collapsible C. To compound matters, steerage passengers were coming down the deck from the stern, and many of them were in a state of great anxiety. They just ran the entire length of the boat deck only to see one empty lifeboat davit after another.

Things changed instantaneously. When C was initially set up and prepared for loading, there were very few people about. Now, the number of people in this area quickly grew to over a hundred. Suddenly a crowd was pressing forward and Wilde and Murdoch found themselves dealing with a potential riot.

Hugh Woolner: "There was a sort of scramble on the starboard side, and I looked around and I saw two flashes of a pistol in the air. But they were up in the air, at that sort of an angle. I heard Mr. Murdoch shouting out, 'Get out of this, clear out of this' and that sort of thing, to a lot of men who were swarming into a boat on that side.

It was a collapsible. On the starboard side. We went across there because we heard a certain kind of shouting going on, and just as we got around the corner I saw these two flashes of the pistol, and Steffanson and I went up to help to clear that boat of the men who were climbing in, because there was a bunch of women - I think Italians and foreigners - who were standing on the outside of the crowd, unable to make their way toward the side of the boat. So we helped the officer to pull these men out, by their legs and anything we could get hold of. I should think five or six. But they were really flying before Mr. Murdoch from inside of the boat at the time. I think they were probably third class passengers. It was awfully difficult to notice very carefully. I got hold of them by their feet and legs, Then they cleared out, practically all the men, out of that boat, and then we lifted in these Italian women, hoisted them up on each side and put them into the boat. Then that boat was finally filled up and swung out."

Senator Smith: "Who fired those two shots?"
Woolner: "Mr. Murdoch, so far as I can tell."
Smith: "You are quite certain it was not Mr. Lowe?"

Woolner: "I am pretty certain. I think I recognized the voice of Mr. Murdoch."

The ship was going down fast now and after the last skirmish, Wilde and Murdoch were in no mood to hold back the boat any longer. Murdoch gave the order to lower away.

Standing alongside one of the davits was Bruce Ismay, Managing Director of the White Star Line. His head must have been reeling. He knew the Titanic was sinking fast. Passengers, and possibly crewmen as well, pushed forward all around him, leaping over the gunwale railing and crashing into several women sitting in the lifeboat. Dangling by ropes along side of the ship, collapsible C rocked in the davits. The officers and crew tried to keep the boat safe as they attempted to get these men out of it at the same time. With the help of some passengers, they grabbed a hold of these men. Fighting broke out. Fists were thrown. People crashed to the deck, wrestling and fighting. Suddenly Murdoch fired his gun. The sound of the gun was deafening, leaving people's ears in the immediate area ringing, including Ismay's. Finally the men were pushed back into the crowd, but everyone continued pressing up near the boat - the last

boat on the starboard side. Glancing over the edge of the ship, Ismay saw the water swirling around the C deck portholes. He saw empty seats in the lifeboat. He knew Chief Officer Wilde, and Ismay knew Wilde would not stop him.

Ismay's blood was racing those final moments. When he heard Murdoch's command to lower away, he could not think about chivalry. The choice between life and death was his to make in that moment. It was now or never, standing there by the side looking at those empty seats going down. Ismay climbed over the railing into the boat. His friend, first class passenger William Carter, saw him make the move and followed. At 2:00 A.M., the man who had a hand in how many lifeboats the Titanic would carry just got off in one.

Ismay: "The ship had quite a list to port. Consequently this canvas boat, this collapsible boat, was getting hung up on the outside of the ship, and she had to rub right along her, and we had to try to shove her out, and we had to get the women to help to shove to get her clear of the ship. The ship had listed over that way."

George Rowe: "All the time my boat was

being lowered the rubbing strake kept on catching on the rivets down the ship's side, and it was as much as we could do to keep her off. When the boat was in the water the well deck was submerged. It took us a good five minutes to lower the boat on account of this rubbing going down."
Senator Burton: "She must have sunk soon after you left?"
Rowe: "Twenty minutes, I believe."

2:00 A.M. was the beginning of the end and the final turning mark for many people, particularly in the lifeboats where they could see the entire length of the Titanic. As collapsible C began its descent, the water crawled over the bow under the railing, then stole along the deck in the shadowy light. While passengers climbed into collapsible D, few on board noticed the water lap along the heavy anchor chains and continue to the base of the first cargo hold. While third class passengers were rushing for the boat deck, the water washed against the forward mast with a sound barely louder than a mild ripple. Only a few feet further and it reached the end of the forecastle deck, splashing up against the railing that overlooked the submerged well deck. The bow of the Titanic went under.

Bruce Ismay and Collapsible C

As with many events throughout time that resulted in eyewitness testimonies, the Titanic disaster has its share of contradictions when it comes to the survivors accounts of things that happened that night. To get close to the truth of what occurred that evening, various accounts should be treated like individual pieces of a puzzle that must be fitted together. When one person's account does not fit into a surrounding number of other accounts, it is a signal that something may be amiss with the account, either because of a faulty memory, embellishment, or personal ulterior motives. The circumstances surrounding Collapsible C and Ismay's departure are shrouded in conflicting testimony ...

Senator Smith: "What were the circumstances of your departure from the ship?"

Bruce Ismay: "The boat was there. There was a certain number of men in the boat, and the officer called out asking if there were any more women, and there was no response, and there were no passengers left on the deck."

Bruce Ismay at the U.S. Senate Inquiry.

Smith: "When you entered the lifeboat yourself, you say there were no passengers on that part of the ship?"
Ismay: "None."
Smith: "Did you at any time see any struggle among the men to get into these boats?"
Ismay: "No."

Hugh Woolner: "... then they got out a collapsible boat and hitched her onto the most forward davits and they filled that up,

mostly with steerage women and children, and one seaman, and a steward, and I think one other man ... There was a sort of scramble on the starboard side, and I looked around and I saw two flashes of a pistol in the air. ... I heard Mr. Murdoch shouting out "Get out of this, clear out of this", and that sort of thing to a lot of men who were swarming into a boat on that side. ... and I went up to help to clear that boat of the men who were climbing in, because there was a bunch of women - I think Italians and foreigners - who were standing on the outside of the crowd, unable to make their way toward the side of the boat."

George Rowe: "At that time they were getting out the starboard collapsible boats ..."
Senator Burton: "Was there any panic that you saw?"
Rowe: "Not a bit."
Burton: "Did you hear any revolver shots?"
Rowe: "No, sir."

Jack Thayer: "There was some disturbance

in loading the last two forward starboard boats. A large crowd of men was pressing to get into them. No women were around as far as I could see. I saw Ismay, who had been assisting in the loading of the last boat, push his way into it. It was really every man for himself... Purser McElroy, as brave and as fine a man as ever lived, was standing up in the next to the last boat, loading it. Two men, I think they were dining room stewards, dropped into the boat from the deck above. As they jumped, he fired twice into the air."

Lightoller: "I may also say, in regard to the testimony in regard to Mr. Ismay, although I can not vouch for the source, yet it was given to me from a source such that I have every reason to believe its truth. It is that Chief Officer Wilde was at the starboard collapsible boat in which Mr. Ismay went away, and that he told Mr. Ismay, "There are no more women on board the ship." Wilde was a pretty big, powerful chap, and he was a man that would not argue very long. Mr. Ismay was right there. Naturally he was there close to the boat, because he was working at the boats and he had been working at the collapsible boat, and that is why he was there, and Mr. Wilde, who was near him, simply bundled him into the boat."

Senator Burton: "Did you see Mr. Ismay and Mr. Carter get in the boat?"
George Rowe: "I saw the gentlemen get in; yes sir."
Burton: "Did you hear anyone ask them to get in?"
Rowe: "No sir."
Burton: "How were you occupied at the time they got in?"
Rowe: "I was occupied in attending the after fall, sir."
Burton: "Were you watching Chief Officer Wilde?"
Rowe: "Yes, sir."
Burton: "Did you see him speak to them?"
Rowe: "No sir."
Burton: "If he had spoken to them would you have known it?"
Rowe: "I think so, because they got in the after part of the boat."

Since virtually all of the survivors on the starboard side stated there were many people in the area when the last collapsible was lowered, any account stating differently should be viewed skeptically. Passengers often spoke of disturbances and gunfire whereas the crew tended to downplay such talk. One never knows for sure with conflicting accounts. But pieced together, it is likely that passengers crowded around collapsible C and the situation became so chaotic that a gun was fired. Under these circumstances, Bruce Ismay climbed aboard the last lifeboat to be lowered on the starboard side.

As Collapsible D hangs over the side ready for loading, the bow of the Titanic slips beneath the surface.

For those who happened to be standing on the forward edge of the upper decks, the sight of Titanic's bow disappearing beneath the dark waters of the Atlantic was clearly a disturbing development. Despite all that had taken place during the last two hours - the loading of the lifeboats, the distress rockets, the noticeable, yet mild slant of the ship forward - despite all signs of danger, the ship at least seemed solid, even if it was down by the head. But now this. Now the bow - that broad stretch of deck in front of the ship, representing a fifth of the ship's length and reaching for almost 200 feet - disappeared beneath the surface.

Just as the command for all passengers to go to the starboard side created problems for Murdoch, the same command created problems for Lightoller as well. Having just prepared collapsible D for launching, there were barely any people about because they were told to go over to the starboard side.

Charles Lightoller: "In the case of the last boat I got out, the very last of all to leave the ship, I had the utmost difficulty in finding women. After all the other boats were put out we came forward to put out the Enghelhardt collapsible boats. Then I called for women and could not get any. Somebody said: 'There are no women'. This was on the Boat Deck where all the women were supposed to be because the boats were there."

It is possible that Lightoller had no other choice at this point but to begin allowing men into the boat during the initial absence of women. Whatever the case, collapsible D was first loaded with men. Unlike Murdoch who followed the rule of women and children first, Lightoller had consistently followed the rule of women and children *only*, regardless of whether he was sending away lifeboats that still had room to take on some men. But with no women or children to be seen anywhere, it clearly would have made no sense to stick to the "no men" rule any longer.

Senator Smith: "Did you have any difficulty in filling it?"
Lightoller: "With women. Yes, sir; great difficulty."
Smith: "But you filled it to its capacity?"
Lightoller: "I filled it with about 15 or 20 eventually mustered up. It took longer to fill that boat than it did any other boat, notwithstanding that the others had more in them. On two occasions the men thought there were no more women and commenced to get in and then found one or two more and then got out again."

Lightoller may not have had a chance to even make the decision of whether to allow men for the first time that night into one of the lifeboats under his charge. Consider the state of mind of the men who were standing near collapsible D. These were men who refused to heed the order to go over to the starboard side to right the ship. In addition, the same thing began to happen on the port side as on the starboard.

Olaus Abelseth: "We stayed a little while longer, and then they said, 'Everybody'. I do not know who that was, but I think it was some of the officers that said it. We went up."

Steerage passengers came running down the boat deck only to find Lightoller's collapsible D to be the last boat left. These men had every intention of getting into that boat if the opportunity afforded itself, and they likely seized the moment and began

When the bow dipped beneath the water around 2:00 A.M. it was a wake up call for many as a large portion of the ship suddenly disappeared. (Olympic)

climbing in from all along the side - with or without the permission of Lightoller.

The second officer was momentarily caught off guard by the lack of women and sudden rush of men arriving from third class.

Harold Bride: "There were other people on deck. They were running around all over the place. Several people looking for life belts and looking for refreshments. The officers' quarters were situated together with the Marconi cabin, the officers' rooms, and other places, and the people were running around through these cabins. We had a woman in our cabin who had fainted. And we were giving her a glass of water there and a chair. We set her down lightly on a chair, which she wanted badly, and then her husband took her away again."

Within moments what had started out as a somewhat orderly loading of the last lifeboat elevated to a borderline panic situation. With the situation getting out of hand, Lightoller ordered a human chain be made around the boat to hold the crowd back. But in the chaos of the situation several steerage men succeeded in climbing in under the bench seats of the boat and hiding in the shadows. John Hardy noticed them later after they were lowered in the water.

John Hardy: "There were a number of third class passengers that were Syrians in the bottom of the boat, chattering the whole night in their strange language."

From the lifeboats, the ship was down by the head and as they watched the final row of porthole lights of the bow disappear, many realized for the first time that the ship was going to sink. Even at this sobering moment,

the liner still glowed brightly across the water and music filtered across the air.

Lawrence Beesley: "The mere bulk alone of the ship nearly a sixth of a mile long, 75 feet high to the top decks, with four enormous funnels above the decks, and masts again high above the funnels; with her hundreds of portholes, all her saloons and other rooms brilliant with light, and all round her, little boats filled with those who until a few hours before had trod her decks and read in her libraries and listened to the music of her band in happy content; and who were now looking up in amazement at the enormous mass above them and rowing away from her because she was sinking."

The Titanic still had a look of greatness, but she was wounded and it was clear now she was dying. The portholes were disappearing one at a time. The roaring steam from the funnels slowed to a trickle and only the third smokestack showed any activity. The first and second stacks were silent and still. The rockets stopped long ago. From the lifeboats, the Titanic was like a patient on a deathbed surrounded by close family.

Although close to foundering now, the Titanic still presented a false impression

to many on board that she was going to float. To others who concluded she was going to sink, there was "still plenty of time" before she did. A look down between the railings of the Grand Staircase would have shown the water not even up to D Deck yet - four whole decks below Boat Deck. Water was seen at the base of the Grand Staircase on E Deck an hour ago and had not even risen one deck since. It was easy to conclude from keeping an eye on the Grand Staircase that the water was barely making any headway.

In addition, a walk through the first class areas at this late hour revealed that the boat deck, along with A, B, and C decks were virtually untouched inside (although the sound of water rushing through open portholes could be heard behind the doors of some of the forward C Deck cabins). Second class was even better off. A walk through that section, which occupied an area two thirds of the way back from the bow, revealed not a drop of water still!

Most in third class heard about other steerage passengers whose cabins in the lower decks of the bow flooded. But the majority of the third class accommodations were in the stern of the ship and that entire area was also completely dry. As the bow sank deeper into the water, the stern actually rose, sending confusing signals to third class. With the water so far away and not coming any closer with the passing of time, it is understandable they allowed themselves to be kept back by the crew during most of the night.

But the apparent lack of progress of the seawater into the passenger areas was very misleading. Boiler rooms 5 and 6 were completely flooded, and 4 was partially submerged. Since it flooded the forward compartments first, the weight of the water pulled the bow of the ship down, which in turn caused the deck areas forward of the Grand Staircase to flood further. By 2:00 A.M. a considerable amount of the bottom and forward part of the ship flooded - away from the view of most passengers.

With hundreds of people crowding the poop and the well decks, there was no possible way to see and hear everything that was going on. If third class passengers were no longer restrained from climbing the stairway to second class, they were not exactly encouraged to go up either. The crew guarding the stairs may have simply walked away and started to think of themselves. This sudden change in circumstances took place in an air of confusion and ignorance. Only those intent on going up may have noticed and taken advantage. Olaus Abelseth indicated he heard the crew finally say "everyone" could go up and he and his cousins did. Other steerage passengers were unaware they were ever allowed to go to the higher decks. Mrs. Rosa Abbott was one of them. Along with her two sons, she stayed at the stern to the very end.

The scores of third class passengers who knew they were allowed up to the boat deck now wandered through the deserted corridors, public rooms, and staircases of the second and first class areas of the Titanic looking for their way to the lifeboats. It would take time - too much time, for some of them. The more athletic and unattached took a direct route by climbing up the ladders located outside on deck. Others attempted to seek out the staircases inside the ship.

Regardless of how the word got around that third class was allowed to go up, a large number of people were set loose into areas of the ship at a critically dangerous period - less than 20 minutes before she sank.

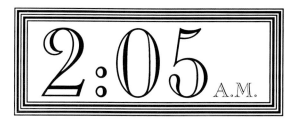

The forward railing on B deck was now dipping underwater. The sea poured over and swirled around the open deck connecting both sides of the ship. Soon the water flooded the walkway and climbed along the forward wall, eventually reaching the first class cabin windows. As they slid under the surface, the light from some of the cabins created a yellowish green glow beneath the ocean foam. The water rose and pressed against two entranceway doors which lead into the B deck corridors of first class. On the other side, seawater trickled through the seams and formed a puddle on the brand new floor.

Down on C Deck, water entered through some open portholes it found into the first class staterooms. As it splashed onto the carpet, it quickly accumulated and rose around the legs of the beds and bureaus. In the hallway just outside, it seeped from under some of the doors and collected at the forward end of the corridor. Slowly, it inched

up the dark and intricately carved wood paneling.

On D Deck, the water crept along the floor of the foyer, eventually coming up on the elevator doors. The elevators were silent now as nobody dared enter them at this late hour. Down the hallway toward the bow where first class staterooms were located, the water progressively deepened until the paneled walls disappeared beneath the green surface. In the opposite direction, around the corner from the elevator, the Reception Room and the Dining Room stood quietly awaiting their fate. Suddenly, there was a huge crash, as stacked dishes somewhere in the kitchen slid off their shelves and fell to the floor. In the abandoned dining room, the sound went unnoticed. The area had been empty of passengers for hours, and the tables stood deserted, waiting for the following days' breakfast crowd that would never come.

On E deck, a good bit of "Scotland Road", the long corridor that ran most of the ship's length, was under water. The water appeared at the foot of the Grand Staircase on this deck around 1:00 A.M.. Then it overflowed down the stairs and flooded the Turkish Bath areas on F deck, and when that was done, it continued its progress along E

deck above. Now, it was 100 feet further up the deck, inching toward the staircases that lead down to the Third Class Dining Saloon on F deck in another watertight compartment. E deck was an important deck because the majority of the watertight bulkheads only went as high as the ceiling of F Deck. It was E Deck that contained access to each of the watertight compartments below. When the water lapped over into the next compartment, it did so from E Deck.

Eventually, the advancing water reached the stairway leading down to the third class dining room. Isolated in a pocket of deck space between the second and third funnels, the third class dining area actually consisted of four separate rooms adjacent to each other located over boiler rooms 2 and 3. The forward two dining rooms were separated from the rear two by a watertight bulkhead with doors which were typically left open for ease of passage during meals. Because of the layout of the staircase entrances from E deck, the water reached the steps going down to the rear dining rooms first.

At a little after two in the morning, the forward pair of dining rooms stood empty, awaiting their destiny. The rooms sat in silence for some time now, ever since third

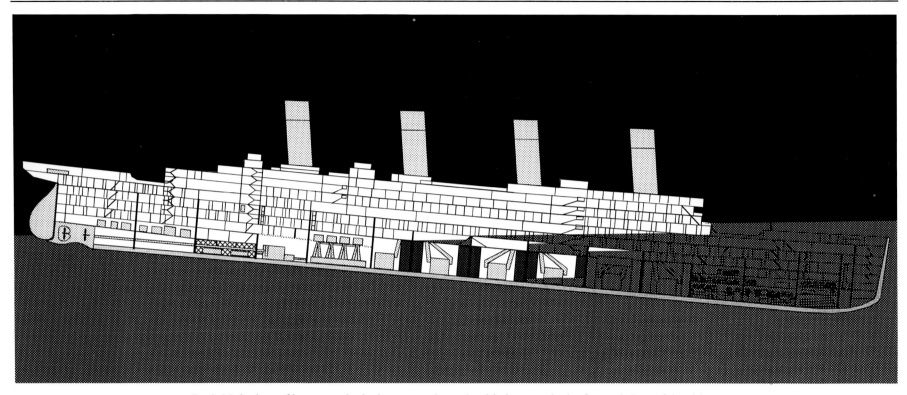

By 2:05 the loss of buoyancy in the bow caused a noticeable increase in the forward slant of the ship.

class passengers, who had gathered to pray after the ship struck the iceberg, left for the higher decks. Somewhere up the stairs, the distant sound of splashing could be heard while the sea poured into the rear dining rooms. Then it started; the water arrived. First came a quiet trickling sound from the steps. The trickle grew to a steady stream with disturbing speed. It came down the steps, spilled across the sloped floor, washing around the legs of the dining room tables and chairs until colliding with the far end of the white enamel wall. The water collected down at the forward end of each dining room and started to rise. It took several minutes, but eventually climbed back up the slant of the floor until it reached the very steps it was pouring in from. The portholes lining the dining room walls once looked out on the Atlantic from one deck above sea level. Now, thirty feet below the dark surface, they looked inward at the room's final moments. The water continued, rising above the chairs which were bolted into the floor at the base of the center swivel. Only a minute or two later, the green water was lapping at the white table cloths, soaking them on contact. It crept along the table surface, immersing the knives, forks, spoons, and plates set in preparation for the third class breakfast. The

Water pours down the staircase from E deck into the third class forward dining saloons.

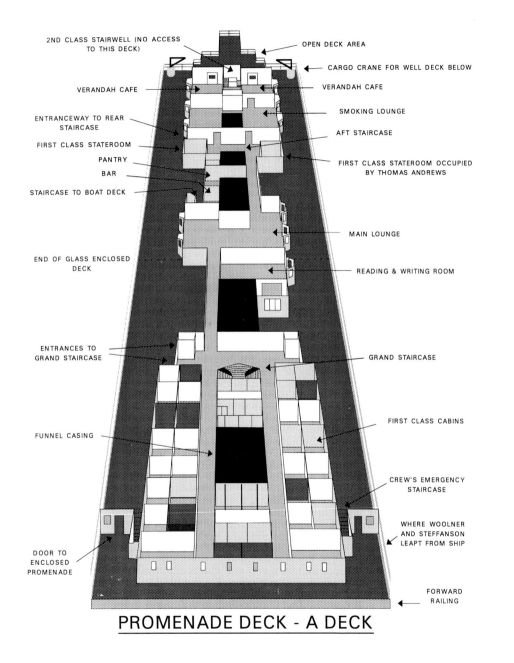

2ND CLASS STAIRWELL (NO ACCESS TO THIS DECK)

OPEN DECK AREA

CARGO CRANE FOR WELL DECK BELOW

VERANDAH CAFE

VERANDAH CAFE

ENTRANCEWAY TO REAR STAIRCASE

SMOKING LOUNGE

AFT STAIRCASE

FIRST CLASS STATEROOM

PANTRY

BAR

FIRST CLASS STATEROOM OCCUPIED BY THOMAS ANDREWS

STAIRCASE TO BOAT DECK

MAIN LOUNGE

END OF GLASS ENCLOSED DECK

READING & WRITING ROOM

ENTRANCES TO GRAND STAIRCASE

GRAND STAIRCASE

FIRST CLASS CABINS

FUNNEL CASING

CREW'S EMERGENCY STAIRCASE

WHERE WOOLNER AND STEFFANSON LEAPT FROM SHIP

DOOR TO ENCLOSED PROMENADE

FORWARD RAILING

PROMENADE DECK - A DECK

entire room would soon be submerged

Unlike the open staircases that lead to the dining rooms, the passageways to the six boiler rooms were not open like a true ice cube tray analogy. Doors concealed the passageways that descended into them. If these doors were closed when the water arrived along E deck, they slowed, if not outright prevented the flooding of the next boiler room below. With access to the next compartment significantly blocked by these doorways, the seawater would have continued its course up the E Deck corridor unobstructed. There is evidence this is exactly what happened that night, as documented by the relatively early appearance of water at the base of the Grand Staircase a little after 1:00 A.M.

The Grand Staircase was situated above boiler room 4. According to trimmer George Cavell, the water did not even begin to appear in boiler room 4 until sometime around 1:30. Even then, it was rising very slowly, giving him time to proceed with his work on the pumps. Eventually, it reached the level of his knees when he decided to evacuate and climb the escape ladder. This ladder lead to two outlets, one on E deck, and the other all the way on A deck. Considering the condition of the ship,

Cavell must have climbed the ladder to A deck.

Once the water reached the Grand Staircase, it made very slow headway along E deck toward the stern, and may have even lost ground at one point, drawing the water back down the deck toward the bow. This was due to the increasing forward tilt of the ship. The more the ship tilted forward, the more the incoming water went toward flooding the bow, specifically C and D decks there.

The comparison between the time the water appeared at the foot of the Grand Staircase versus when it appeared in boiler room 4 documents that F, and then E decks filled with water before boiler room 4 directly beneath. George Cavell's account indicates the slow pace at which boiler room 4 was flooding. It is not clear where this water was coming from but there are several possibilities. One is that water under pressure began forcing its way through the closed E deck door leading to the boiler room. Another is that a pipe connecting a forward boiler room with the engine room aft may have broken under pressure. A third possibility is that the water was coming through some early but minor cracking in the forward bulkhead, symptomatic of the

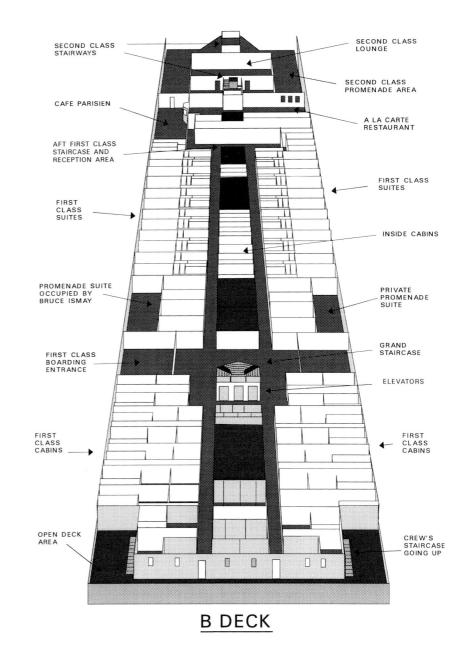

B DECK

catastrophic failure of the structure about to occur from the immense pressure that was building up on this watertight compartment.

Because incoming water had easier access to E and F Decks than it did to the boiler rooms below, this type of flooding reduced the Titanic's ability to remain on an even keel. It created a condition where water was resting on top of air. The air in the unflooded boiler rooms below exerted pressure on to the ship to rise. At the same time, the water directly above on E and F Decks exerted a pressure on the ship to sink. The two opposing forces created a rotating force on the balance of the ship, explaining the persistent and increasing lean of the ship to port, particularly toward the end.

Archibald Gracie: "When we were loading the last boat, just a short time before it was fully loaded, a palpable list toward the port side began, and the officer called out, 'All passengers to the starboard side', and (Clinch) Smith and myself went to the starboard side, still at the bow of the ship."

Up on the port side of the boat deck, Lightoller continued loading collapsible D slowly. Incredibly, there were still women over on the starboard side even though collapsible C had just been sent away. This was attributable to the ongoing arrival of steerage class passengers who had been released from the stern. One by one they were ushered over to the edge of the boat deck and hoisted over the gunwale into collapsible D. Beneath them, the forward B deck cabin windows were under water, casting the same eerie glow seen all over the Titanic at the waterline. The water was now lapping around the base of the Promenade Deck just one deck below. Time was extremely short.

Jack Phillips, the wireless operator, decided to come out of the wireless room on the port side and have a look around the Boat Deck. He had been busy sending out the call for assistance for the last two hours and wanted to see for himself how things were. The ship was leaning forward and to the port. The lights were still blazing, although the waning power on board created a reddish hue around them. There were a lot of people about but there was only one lifeboat. Most people were standing behind the human chain that had been formed, watching it being loaded. Others were eyeing Samuel Hemming up on the roof near the first funnel, waiting for some progress on releasing collapsible B, tied down there. Phillips went over to the edge of the boat deck, where he must have been stunned to see the water crawling over the B deck square windows. He leaned further over the edge and followed the waterline forward to the base of the promenade deck. Disturbed by what he saw, he walked back across the boat deck and inside the wireless cabin.

Harold Bride: "He told us he thought it was time we put on our life belts. Mr. Phillips told me that things looked very queer outside. Beyond that I knew nothing. Mr. Phillips sat down again at the telephones and gave a general call of CQD, but I think that our lamps were running down; we did not get a spark. We could not tell, because the spark of our wireless was in an enclosed room. We could not hear at any time whether it was sparking."

Little did they know, but the steamship *Virginian* heard the Titanic's final call for assistance but noted that the signal ended very abruptly. The "spark" died right in the middle of the transmission. The world had heard the last from the Titanic.

Although dedicated to the end,

Phillips had no intention of going down with the ship trapped inside the small wireless room. He and Bride prepared to abandon the wireless cabin.

Bride: " On Mr. Phillips request I started to gather up his spare money and put on another coat, and made general preparations for leaving the ship. We had to wait until the captain told us first."

With more steerage passengers arriving every moment, Lightoller suddenly found himself under siege by all of these people trying to get into the last lifeboat. The human chain that he had the crew form was not holding and men began breaking through the line and jumping into the boat. Lightoller fired a warning shot into the air.

Archibald Gracie: "As to what happened on the other side (port side) during our departure, the information I was given by the second officer was that some of the steerage passengers tried to rush the boat, and he fired off a pistol to make them get out, and they did get out.
Senator Smith: "Who fired that pistol?"
Gracie: "Lightoller. That is what he told me. He is the second officer."

Smith: "Are you sure it was not Murdoch?"
Gracie: " I am sure it was not Murdoch".
Smith: "Or Lowe?"
Gracie: "I am sure it was not. That is what Mr. Lightoller himself told me. I did not hear the pistol. That is what I was told by Lightoller himself. That is all hearsay, Senator."

Archibald Gracie crossed over to the starboard side, probably across the open deck amidship between the second and third funnels. This was a raised deck area positioned over the First Class Lounge and the short stairs on the starboard side were located just aft of the gymnasium and near the empty davits of where lifeboat number 7 had hung. Just aft of this davit, the edge of the boat deck was protected with a gunwale and railing that ran toward the stern for half the deck up to the rear lifeboats. Here, Gracie arrived on the starboard side.

Gracie: "All the lifeboats had been lowered and had departed. There was somewhat of a crowd congregated along the rail. The light was sufficient for me to recognize distinctly many of those with whom I was well acquainted. Here, pale and determined, was Mr. John B. Thayer, Second Vice President of the Pennsylvania Railroad, and Mr. George D. Widener. They were looking over the ship's gunwale, talking earnestly as if debating what to do. Next to them it pained me to discover Mrs. J.M. Brown and Miss Evans, the two ladies whom more than an hour previous I had consigned to the care of Sixth Officer Moody on Deck A, where he ... blocked my purpose of accompanying these ladies and personally assisting them into the boat. They showed no signs of perturbation whatever as they conversed quietly with me. Mrs. Brown quickly related how they became separated in the crowd from her sisters, Mrs. Appleton and Mrs. Cornell. Alas! That they had not remained on the same port side of the ship, or moved forward on Deck A, or the Boat Deck! Instead, they had wandered in some unexplained way to the very furthest point diagonally from where they were at first. At the time of introduction, I had not caught Miss Evans' name and when we were here together at this critical moment I thought it important to ask, and she gave me her name. Meantime the crew were working on the roof of the officers' quarters to cut loose one of the Engelhardt boats. All this took place more quickly than it takes to write it.
During this very short interval I was

on the starboard side, as described, next to the rail, with Mrs. Brown and Miss Evans, when I heard a member of the crew, coming from the quarter where the last boat was loaded, say that there was room for more ladies in it. I immediately seized each lady by the arm, and with Miss Evans on my right and Mrs. Brown on my left, hurried, with three other ladies following us, toward the port side; but I had not proceeded half-way, and near amidship, when I was stopped by the aforesaid line of the crew barring my progress, and one of the officers told me that only the women could pass."

These two women seemed uninterested in getting into a lifeboat. It is possible that Edith Evans was petrified at the thought of climbing into one of the boats and that Caroline Brown, in attempting to comfort her, agreed to stay by her side. An additional clue is furnished after Gracie handed them off amidship.

Lightoller: "On the port side on deck, I can say, as far as my own observations went, from my own endeavor and that of others to obtain women, there were none. I can give you the name of a man who will give testimony, who was working with me, one of

The area just outside the gymnasium where Gracie found Caroline Brown and Edith Evans. (Olympic)

our best men, a man I picked out especially to man the falls for lowering away. He went from the port side to the starboard side of the deck, as I did and after that, when she went under water forward, instead of taking to the water, he walked aft the whole length of the boat deck previous to sliding down the aft fall on the port side, and in the whole length of the deck and in crossing the bridge he saw two women. They were standing amidship on the bridge perfectly still. They

did not seem to be endeavoring to get to one side or the other to see if there were any boats or not."

Gracie attempted to figure out why Caroline Brown managed to survive but Edith Evans did not.

Gracie: "The story of what now happened to Mrs. Brown and Miss Evans after they left me must be told by Mrs. Brown, as related to me by herself when I rejoined her next on board the Carpathia. Miss Evans led the way, she said, as they neared the rail where what proved to be the last lifeboat was being loaded, but in a spirit of most heroic self-sacrifice, Miss Evans insisted upon Mrs. Brown taking precedence in being assisted aboard the boat. "You go first" she said. "You are married and have children". But when Miss Evans attempted to follow after, she was unable to do so for some unknown cause. The women in the boat were not able, it would appear, to pull Miss Evans in. It was necessary for her first to clear the four feet high ship's gunwale, and no man or member of the crew was at this particular point to lift her over. I have questioned Mr. Lightoller several times about this, but he has not been able to give any satisfactory explanation and cannot understand it, for when he gave orders to lower away, there was no woman in sight. Perhaps what I have read in a letter of Mrs. Brown may furnish some reason why Miss Evans' efforts to board the lifeboat, in which there was plenty of room for her, were unavailing. "Never mind' she is said to have called out, 'I will go on a later boat'. She then ran away and was not seen again; but there was no later boat, and it would seem that after a momentary impulse, being disappointed and being unable to get into the boat, she went aft on the port side, and no one saw her again."

The fact that Brown was escorted into the lifeboat and Evans was not is odd and implies the truth of the matter is that Evans never even reached the side of the lifeboat in the first place. It also implies that in the end, Brown may have had an interest in getting into a lifeboat all along and Evans never did. Standing on the bridge, Brown may have attempted one last time to get Evans to go with her into a lifeboat. Evans may have started feeling guilty about Brown remaining on the Titanic on her account and decided to accompany her to the boat only to duck back into the crowd once there. Brown reached the boat only seconds before it was lowered only to turn around and find that Evans was nowhere to be seen. Standing alongside the collapsible, Brown may have been ordered, or physically forced into the boat at this point.

Olaus Abelseth: "We went over to the port side of the ship and there were just one or two boats on the port side that were left. Anyway, there was one. We were standing there looking at them lowering this boat. We could see them, some of the crew helping take the ladies in their arms and throwing them into the lifeboats."

Archibald Gracie's account highlights the state of things. Even though the last lifeboat was about to be lowered, five women just on the other side of the boat deck seemed unaware of this until personally told. And when one of the women had some sort of difficulty getting in - either from fear or some other reason, there was no focused attention by the crew in helping her. It is likely that if Lightoller had to use his gun to fire warning shots, then there was a chaotic crowd surrounding and threatening the boat. There was no time left to pamper anyone.

After passengers were seated in the lifeboat, it seems they no longer had a good view of the boat deck. Members of the crew who were assisting with the collapsible lifeboat mentioned it.

Senator Fletcher: "But did any ladies refuse to get in that boat - that last boat - any who were asked to get in?"
Arthur Bright: "Not to my knowledge."
Fletcher: "Were there some there?"

Bright: "I did not see any when that boat went out."

Fletcher: "It was dark?"

Bright: "My attention was elsewhere. I was looking after the boat getting clear. You see they got the boat clear of the ship and then the people were put in afterwards."

Fletcher: "And you were on board the boat?"

Bright: "Yes, keeping her in an upright position to save the people from falling into the water."

Fletcher: "And Mr. Lightoller and several others were helping the passengers in, you have said. Did they call out for anybody to come there?"

Bright: "No; I could not hear."

To Lightoller, there was an incredible pressure to get the lifeboat into the water and away from the ship. The water was not even two decks below him now and rising fast. There was a growing crowd of steerage passengers and crew being held back by a ring of men locking arms which could unravel into a panic and a rush on the collapsible lifeboat at any moment.

Just about this time, Chief Officer Wilde walked over from the starboard side where collapsible C had just been lowered and where they were now working on getting collapsible A off the roof and set up in the davits. Wilde had mainly provided general supervision of the lifeboat evacuation, whereas Murdoch and Lightoller were directly in charge of their lowering. Getting collapsible A launched in time was probably a long shot in Wilde's mind. As he passed through the bridge crossing over from starboard to port, he could see that the water was only a deck below. Coming up on collapsible D with 25 people in it, he knew it had to be lowered immediately if it was to get away safely. John Hardy was sitting in the boat assisting Lightoller with the loading of the passengers.

John Hardy: "When the boat was full, Mr. Lightoller was in the boat with me and the chief officer came along and asked if the boat was full, and he said yes. He said he would step out himself and make room for somebody else, and he stepped back on board the ship and asked if I could row. I told him I could, and I went away in that boat."

Interestingly enough, Hardy mentions a little later in his testimony that Lightoller was still in the boat when it was being lowered.

Senator Fletcher: "... when you lowered away from the ship did you take all that she would hold safely or all who were there?"

Hardy: "We took all who were there. There was nobody to lower the afterfall until Mr. Lightoller went aboard to do it himself."

Fletcher: "Were there passengers on board the ship standing there trying to get on board the lifeboat?"

Hardy: "There was nobody on board, because we could not get our collapsible boat lowered from one end of it. The forward part of the collapsible boat was lowered, but there was nobody there to lower the after end, which you will find in Mr. Bright's evidence. Mr. Lightoller stepped from the collapsible boat aboard the ship again and did it himself."

This bit of testimony from Hardy is mysterious for two reasons. First, Hardy says there was nobody in the area when the boat was being lowered. Yet, in reality there were plenty of men in the area hoping for a seat on the boat. In fact there were so many men that a human gate was formed to keep them back from the boat. Lightoller was

Chief Officer Henry Wilde.

Second Officer Charles Lightholler

Hardy's observation that there were no people around was based upon the *immediate* area within several feet of the railing. If Hardy was sitting down in the lifeboat, just like Bright, he would not have had a good view of the general boat deck area.

Another interesting aspect of Hardy's testimony is that he comments two separate times that Lightoller was still inside the lifeboat when collapsible D actually started descending by the forward fall. According to Hardy, Lightoller got out of the boat only when it became apparent there was nobody to man the aft fall of the boat. It should also be noted that he states that Lightoller stepped from the collapsible aboard the ship *again*. This use of the word "again" suggests that Lightoller got out of the collapsible, then got back into it, then got out of it "again". Years later in his book, Lightoller gave his account.

Lightoller: "I stood partly in the boat, owing to the difficulty of getting womenfolk over a high bulwark rail just here. As we were ready for lowering the Chief came over to my side of the deck and, seeing me in the boat and no seaman available said, 'You go with her Lightoller'. Praises be, I

questioned by Senator Smith later about why he did not load more people into the boats with 1,500 people still on board. If there had been no one in the area, Lightoller would have seized the opportunity to make that point to the senator - but he did not. Instead, he testified that he loaded the boats up to the capacity he thought safe. In addition, he made a point to state that there was a problem in locating women for the last collapsible lifeboat - but never mentioned a shortage of men. Perhaps

had just sufficient sense to say, 'Not damn likely.' and jump back on board."

Piecing together the accounts of these two men, it appears the following sequence occurred during the final moments before collapsible D was lowered. Standing in the lifeboat assisting with the loading, Chief Officer Wilde walks up to the boat and asks the status. Lightoller is standing in the boat and chooses this time to climb out of it and tell Wilde it is ready to go. Wilde

The location of the ship where collapsible D was lowered.

descent again.

To the passengers of Collapsible D, the sound of orders to lower away must have been a relief. Hanging along the side of the ship in the shadows, they could see the ship very noticeably sinking. They knew the situation on the boat deck was growing desperate. The Titanic was still leaning over to the port side, but the severity of the list in that direction had lessened once the bow went under water.

The lifeboat began to descend. The first and only deck it passed by was the Promenade Deck. Just before they came down alongside it, Frederick Hoyt jumped from one of its opened windows into the water.

Frederick Hoyt: "I knew Captain Smith for over fifteen years. Our conversation that night amounted to little or nothing. I simply sympathized with him on the accident; but at that time, as I then never expected to be saved, I did not want to bother him with questions, as I knew he had all he wanted to think of. He did suggest that I go down to A deck and see if there were not a boat alongside. This I did, and to my surprise saw the boat 'D' still hanging on the davits and it occurred to me that if I swam out and waited

tells Lightoller that since there are no seamen in the boat, that Lightoller is to go with the collapsible. Lightoller climbs back into the lifeboat and Wilde orders the boat away. But something goes wrong. There are not enough experienced men around to lower the boat. Wilde may be working the forward falls himself. The man assigned to lower the aft falls does not know what he is doing and the

ropes remain still. As a result, the forward end of the boat begins to descend, and the aft does not. Lightoller is not comfortable with going away in the lifeboat in the first place and seizes this opportunity to jump back on board to work the aft falls. At this point, he questions Hardy if he knows how to row, and when Hardy says he does, that's enough to satisfy Lightoller and the boat begins its *for her to shove off they would pick me up, which was what happened."*

Only seconds after Hoyt jumped out one of the windows, Hugh Woolner and Bjornstom Steffanson came out the doorway from the Grand Staircase foyer. Collapsible D was just beginning to descend and they probably heard Lightoller or Wilde's distant voice from the deck above yell out, "Lower away!" Collapsible D was in such a position that the rear of the lifeboat was alongside the Promenade Deck windows and the front of the boat was alongside an open portion of the deck.

Hugh Woolner: "... the electric lights along the ceiling of A deck were beginning to turn red, just a glow, a red sort of glow. So I said to Steffanson: 'this is getting rather a tight corner. I do not like being inside these closed windows. Let us go out through the door at the end.' And as we went out through the door the sea came in onto the deck at our feet. Then we hopped up onto the gunwale preparing to jump out into the sea, because if we had waited a minute longer we should have been boxed in against the ceiling. And as we looked out we saw this collapsible, the last boat on the port side, being lowered

As Collapsible D nears the water, Hugh Woolner prepares to jump into its bow from the forward end of the Titanic's Promenade Deck.

right in front of our faces. It was full up to the bow, and I said to Steffanson: 'There is nobody in the bows. Let us make a jump for it. You go first.' And he jumped out and tumbled in head over heels into the bow, and I jumped too, and hit the gunwale with my chest, which had on this life preserver, of course, and I sort of bounced off the gunwale and caught the gunwale with my fingers, and

slipped off backwards. As my legs dropped down I felt that they were in the sea. Then I hooked my right heel over the gunwale, and by this time Steffanson was standing up, and he caught hold of me and lifted me in. Then we looked over into the sea and saw a man swimming in the sea just beneath us, and pulled him in. By that time we were bumping against the side of the ship. She was going

49

Water pours over the forward railing of A deck as the last lifeboat is lowered from the Titanic.

down pretty fast by the bow. We were exactly opposite the end of the glass windows on the A deck."

With water pouring over the railing nearby, Collapsible D was in considerable danger of being drawn into the forward open area of A Deck. Quickly, the passengers and crew of the boat took three oars, put them up against the side of the Titanic and pushed off.

The passengers and crew on the port side were now standing around an empty davit. There were no other lifeboats except for collapsible B still tied down on the roof of the officers quarters. The ship was still leaning stubbornly to port despite several orders for the passengers to move over to starboard. As Lightoller headed for the ladder that lead up to the roof of the officers quarters, Captain Smith appeared.

Senator Smith: "Tell us, as nearly as you can, just where you saw the captain last, with reference to the sinking ship.
Lightoller: "I think the bridge was the last place I saw him, sir; I am not sure. I think he was crossing the bridge."
Smith: "From one side to the other?"
Lightoller: "No, sir; just coming across. I merely recognized a glimpse. I have a slight recollection of having seen him whilst I was walking.
Smith: "When you saw him was he giving any orders?"
Lightoller: "I was not near enough to know, sir."
Smith: "How near were you?"
Lightoller: "About 50 feet away."
Smith: "What did he seem to be doing - pacing?"
Lightoller: "No, sir; not pacing. Just walking straight across, as if he had some object that he was walking toward."
Smith: "He was walking from one side to the other?"
Lightoller: "Yes, sir; from starboard to port."

It is interesting to note that based on various accounts, Captain Smith, Chief Officer Wilde, and Second Officer Lightoller should have been in the same general location on the port side of the boat deck at this point. But Lightoller testified at the Senate Inquiry that he never spoke with the captain after his initial orders to lower away the lifeboats a little after midnight. The fact that he had no further discussion with the other two men just before the ship sank highlights how fast things were moving.

Captain Smith, concerned about the stubborn lean to port, was probably on his way to the wing of the port bridge to see just how close the water was getting. He may have even been curious to find out if his suggestion to Frederick Hoyt worked out. Lightoller, finished with his duties launching the boats, stated in his own words that he was on his way somewhere and was not "near enough to know" if the captain had issued any final order. Perhaps he momentarily ducked inside his quarters to round up some of his personal belongings, or was busy climbing onto the roof of the officers quarters to work on collapsible B. It is not clear where Wilde headed after that. Evidently the three of them did not choose that final moment together to wish each other luck or to say goodbye.

Samuel Hemming was working on collapsible B still tied to the roof of the officers' quarters. The collapsible was tied down with ropes and Hemming may not have had a knife because he left the roof. Leaning over the forward railing of the bridge in the meantime, the captain watched the water swirling around the port side of A deck just below. As Hemming jumped back down to the boat deck he was just in time to hear what was probably Captain Smith's final order.

Hemming: "The captain was there and he sung out: 'Everyone over to the starboard side to keep the ship up as long as possible!'"

Hemming followed the captains orders and went over to the starboard side, soon to work on collapsible A. Wilde probably went over with him. Knowing that the ship was about to founder, the captain headed for the boat deck door nearby that lead to the wireless office to relieve the operators from their duty.

Senator Smith: "How did you expect to leave the ship?"

Harold Bride: "We had to wait until the captain told us first. He came along in a very short period afterwards and told us we had better look out for ourselves."

Smith: "Where was he when he had said this?"

Bride: "He came around to the cabin to tell us."

In a newspaper interview, Bride elaborated a little more.

Bride:"Then came the Captain's voice: 'Men you have done your full duty. You can do no more. Abandon your cabin. Now it's every man for himself.'"

The water continued over the railing onto A deck. It swirled about the teak deck and climbed the freshly painted white walls facing forward. It went around the corner and along the door to the crew's staircase, which lead from boat to B deck. It rose along the deck and met the doors leading into the glass enclosed promenade. Time was running out.

The Ship on the Horizon - Part II

Nagging Inconsistencies

For all of the evidence against the Californian, there are, on the other hand, three important inconsistencies in the eyewitness accounts which do not add up if the Californian was the ship on the horizon. Nothing has ever surfaced to discount these inconsistencies. They are strong points in supporting the theory that the Californian was too far away at the time and that there must have been another ship in between.

From the Titanic
Senator Smith: "What lights did you see?"
Boxhall: "The two masthead lights and the red light."

From the Californian
Gill: "I had been on deck about 10 minutes when I saw a white rocket about 10 miles away on the starboard side."

This is the first inconsistency. Ships carried side lights to indicate which direction they were traveling in to other ships. A green light indicated the ship's starboard side, a red one for the port side. If Boxhall saw the red light, that would have indicated the Californian's *port side* was facing the Titanic. However, Gill states that he saw the rockets off the Californian's *starboard side.*

From the Titanic
Senator Fletcher: "Apparently that ship came within 4 or 5 miles of the Titanic, and then turned and went away in what direction, westward or southward?"
Boxhall: "I do not know that it was southwestward. I should say westerly."

From the Californian
Captain Lord: "... this steamer had steamed away from us to the southwest, showing several of these flashes or white rockets."

This is the second inconsistency. If both ships were watching each other from a distance, how could they both see each other sail off to the west? This is impossible. However, it would make sense if they were both watching a third boat in between them.

From the Californian
Gill: "... I thought it must be a shooting star. In seven or eight minutes I saw distinctly a second rocket in the same place and I said to myself, 'That must be a vessel in distress'. I turned in immediately afterwards."
Fletcher: "Did you see any lights on the steamer where the rockets were sent up?"
Gill: "No, sir; no sign of the steamer at the time."

This is a third inconsistency.

Boxhall never mentioned being unable to see the lights of the distant ship while firing rockets, yet Gill states that he could only see the rockets in the air, and not the ship. This implies that the Titanic was so far away that Gill could not see her because she was way over the horizon.

These three inconsistencies, and especially the first two, have been the foundation for why the ship on the horizon has gone down in history as the mystery ship. All obvious accounts strongly implicate the Californian. But there are these three nagging inconsistencies which have kept the discussion open for almost a century.

No evidence has ever come forward to prove or discount the weight of these points. The theory of a third ship between the Titanic and Californian has been offered up as an explanation and answer to the inconsistencies but no boat has ever been documented as being in the location between the two ships at the time of the disaster.

It must be continuously remembered that this was first and foremost a human tragedy. The accounts and observations were all offered by people - and people make mistakes. The following is an example. In this case, Lookout Frederick Fleet was on duty in the crows nest and was the person who first sighted the iceberg.

Senator Burton: "You say it (the iceberg) struck the port bow, 50 feet from the bow?" Frederick Fleet: "Yes sir."

Here, the very lookout who witnessed the iceberg strike the starboard side of the Titanic tells Senator Burton that he is correct when he states the iceberg struck the port bow. Many of these small types of errors probably occurred in the accounts, which is why so many inconsistencies exist on topics pertaining to that night. Could somebody have made an error when testifying, particularly about which side of the ship they had seen? Since the Californian was drifting that night, is it possible that Stone and Gibson were so intent on watching the Titanic that they did not take note of the motion of their own ship? Thinking they were looking south originally, is it possible that the Californian was drifting around in a circle and they mistook the distant lights moving across their field of view as evidence that it was steaming away to the southwest?

This discussion must return to one key point time and again. The crew of the Californian testified themselves that they could see distress rockets being fired directly above the ship on the horizon - eight rockets - the exact same number that the Titanic fired. Would the Californian have been able to save anybody if they had set out for the Titanic after seeing the first distress rocket?

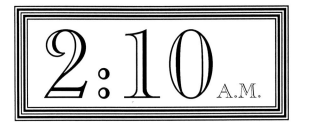
2:10 A.M.

Attention now turned to collapsible lifeboats A and B tied down to the roof of the officers quarters at the base of the first funnel, one on each side. Crewmen were working on untying the ropes for an awfully long time considering the condition of the ship and the prospect of these two boats getting launched in time was becoming a long shot. While they worked, passengers below who just watched collapsible D launched on the boat deck obeyed the

First Class Cabin C9. Sometime after 2:00 water seeped under the door and across the floor.

captains orders and crossed over to the starboard side, joining hundreds already there.

It was now 2:10 A.M. The Titanic's bow was twenty to thirty feet under the surface. The water swirled about the forward end of A deck, looking for a way into the enclosed promenade area. The liner was holding up well considering how much upper deck space was submerged. Even though the forward end of A, B, and C decks were now submerged on the outside, the interior was not so easy to enter. And in those areas where the water could access the ship, like open portholes and windows, it was slowed by closed stateroom doors.

On D deck, the water advanced into the Reception Room and then slowed to a creep. As it lapped around the base of the Grand Staircase, it lost its forward momentum altogether and came to a temporary stop. The water was still pouring down the staircase below into the F deck dining saloon for third class, effectively draining off any advance on the higher decks. As a result, there was a momentary calm in the Reception Room at 2:10 in the morning. It was quiet down on D deck and the ceiling lights reflected elegantly off the placid surface of the dark green water that crept into

the room. Earlier that evening the men and women of first class retired to this room after dinner and listened to the orchestra while enjoying an after dinner drink. It was also known as the Palm Room and was one of the most popular rooms on board (the company had this room enlarged from the original plans after observing its popularity on the sister ship Olympic). After the Titanic struck the iceberg and the engines stopped, some of the passengers came to this room to await news. Now the room was deserted and a strange tranquility set in for the few remaining minutes, interrupted only by an occasional creaking sound emanating from somewhere in the ship.

First Class Cabin C15.

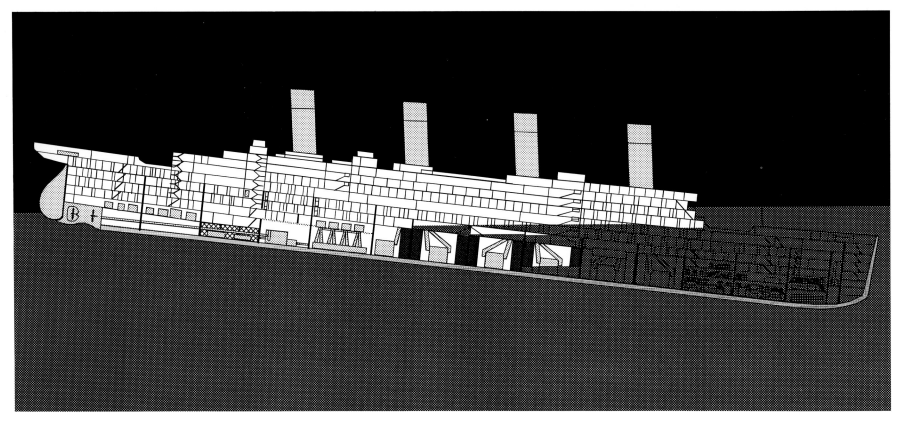

By 2:10 the Titanic corrected itself for the loss of buoyancy in the bow and momentarily slowed its forward lean.

When the bow of the Titanic went under, a considerable amount of its forward buoyancy was lost, and the ship underwent a correction in its distribution of weight. As a result, a noticeable slanting motion was detected by the passengers at this time:

Jack Thayer: "Long and I debated whether or not we should fight our way into one of the last two boats. We could almost see the ship slowly going down by the head."

Once the correction ran its course, the outside of the ship was under water all the way up to A deck. But the inside of the upper decks remained relatively dry, allowing the

Titanic to enjoy a brief reprieve for several minutes as she regained some forward buoyancy. This explains why the water rose at such an alarming speed right up to the A deck promenade during the loading of collapsible D, then paused another five minutes or more before overtaking the bridge just one deck higher. This momentary

Water creeps around the foot of the Grand Staircase in the first class Reception Room.

slowing may have instilled some faith in those still hopeful that the ship would somehow stay afloat. Only minutes before the Titanic began her final plunge, some passengers and crew still seemed unaware of the severity of the situation.

Archibald Gracie: "Two young men of the crew, nice looking, dressed in white, one tall and the other smaller, were coolly debating as to whether the compartments would hold the ship afloat. They were standing with their backs to the rail looking on at the rest of the crew, and I recall asking one of them why he did not assist."

The weight of the water on the submerged cargo hatches of the forecastle and well decks was building fast and before long they would cave in. In addition, water was having a difficult time working its way into the aft boiler rooms fast enough to keep pace with the incoming flow, while having a much easier time flowing unimpeded along E and F decks aft. This process of flooding created an incredible pressure against the front and top of the remaining boiler rooms, particularly boiler room number 4. The Titanic had a pressure fuse building inside her which was about to set off a catastrophic plunge forward, taking everyone by surprise.

Of the approximate 1,500 people on board at this point, only 50 or so would survive based on the choices they made in the coming minutes. Some were aware of the danger and thinking how they could save themselves under the circumstances. Others were aware of the approaching end, but vague about what to do next. Still others were uninformed or fooling themselves into thinking (or not thinking at all) that nothing needed to be done except to stay at the highest part of the ship until help arrived from another vessel.

Mrs. J. Stuart White: "Nobody ever thought the ship was going down. I do not think there was a person that night, I do not think there was a man on the boat who thought the ship was going down. They speak of the bravery of the men. I do not think there was any particular bravery because none of the men thought it was going down. If they had thought the ship was going down, they would not have frivoled as they did about it."

Obviously, Mrs. White's comments cannot be applied to everyone, or for the entire period of the sinking. However, even at this late hour, how many people still realized the severity of the situation, particularly when they could not see the condition of the boat as those in the lifeboats could see it? In only a few minutes the Titanic was going to take a plunge forward, stand on end, and be completely gone - dumping everybody left on board into 28 degree Fahrenheit water. Although a good many may have concluded by this point that the ship was going to sink, an equal number on board still thought the Titanic was just settling to a point where the "unsinkable watertight compartments" would keep the ship afloat.

Senator Newlands: "What was the feeling among the crew as to whether the ship would sink or not?"
W. H. Taylor: "A majority of them did not realize that she would sink."
Newlands: "Was that ship regarded by the crew as an unsinkable ship?"
Taylor: "So they thought."
Newlands: "Regarding these great iron ships, with watertight compartments, that is the general feeling among the seamen, is it?"
Taylor: "Yes sir."
Newlands: "They feel safe on them?"
Taylor: "Yes."

Newlands: *"Even although there are not enough boats to accommodate all the crew and passengers?"*
Taylor: *"Yes, sir."*
Newlands: *"Did you ever hear that matter discussed among them?"*
Taylor: *"No sir"*
Newlands: *"Then how do you know that that is the feeling?"*
Taylor: *"Because they were all skylarking and joking about it."*
Newlands: *"After the accident were they joking about it?"*
Taylor: *"Yes sir."*
Newlands: *"If they had realized that there was serious danger, there would have been a terrible scene there, would there not?"*
Taylor: *"Yes, sir; everybody would have been rushing for their lives."*
Newlands: *"When you got on to the boat did you feel that it was safer in the boat, or remaining on the ship?"*
Taylor: *"I thought it was safer for us in the boat."*
Newlands: *"Why did you think so?"*
Taylor: *Because I saw her then going down by the nose."*
Newlands: *"You realized then that she was sinking?"*
Taylor: *"After we got clear of her we could see her going down by the bow."*
Newlands: *"But you did not realize that at the time you got into the lifeboat?"*
Taylor: *"No sir; I only thought we were getting in in case there was an emergency."*

Taylor left in lifeboat 15, one of the last lowered and less than an hour before the ship sank. Still, he was under the impression there was no danger until he was able to see the condition of the ship objectively from a distance. John Hardy left even later in collapsible D, the last lifeboat to be lowered that night. He had faith in the ship right to the end.

Senator Fletcher: *"Was there anything like a panic on board the ship?"*
Hardy: *"Not at all, because everybody had full confidence that the ship would float."*
Fletcher: *"Up to what time? Up to the time your boat left?"*
Hardy: *"Up to the time my boat left."*

It is likely that this type of false security remained on the boat right up to the time the ship took a plunge.

At 2:10 A.M. there were few choices available. One could stay at the forward end of the boat deck in hopes of getting a seat on collapsible A or B, which were not even set up in the davits yet. One could head for the stern of the ship which was further above the water and becoming increasingly more crowded. Or one could basically do nothing and simply wait on time. It is likely an equal number of people on the ship chose each option. For those who concluded the Titanic was definitely going to founder, their course of action was based upon what they had heard about the dangers of a sinking ship.

Most experienced with the sea knew that it was not wise to stay with a sinking ship to the end because of the notorious suction. It was a widespread belief that when a ship went down, particularly the largest ship in the world, she would suck down everything nearby with her to the bottom of the ocean. Many others were unaware of this information and planned to stay toward the highest part of the ship for as long as possible. To them, it made no sense to jump into the water sooner than necessary. These people for the most part began collecting in large numbers toward the stern.

Those that took the situation seriously were at the forward end of the boat deck. Their chances for survival were best there because they could try and get into one of the remaining collapsible lifeboats, and if that didn't work, they could jump from the ship early enough to avoid the suction when the water reached the stern.

The band had been playing upbeat ragtime music for almost two hours while the lifeboats were loaded before them. With the last lifeboat gone and the ship far down by the bow, the band struck up yet another ragtime tune, called Songe d'Automne. It would be their last piece and serve as the Titanic's swan song. Known generally by the British public as "Autumn" it drifted along the port side of the boat deck and out across the water.

As Bride came out on deck from the small wireless cabin, the sound of the music struck his senses enough that he took note of the song in his memory. According to Bride, he and Phillips then parted ways. This seems a bit odd, since the two worked so closely side by side throughout the voyage, and particularly that evening during the crisis. In the New York Times interview later, he went so far as to say of Phillips ...

Bride: "I learned to love him that night, and I suddenly felt for him a great reverence to see him standing there sticking to his work while everybody else was raging about."

Considering the circumstances, it seems they would have felt some sort of comraderie to look out for each other as they walked out onto the crowded boat deck with the ship about to go down. But instead, Phillips immediately turned and headed up the deck and Bride headed toward the officers quarters where efforts were underway to get collapsible B off the roof.

Time was critically short and progress toward getting the two collapsible lifeboats set up in the davits for loading passengers was moving at a painstakingly slow pace.

Archibald Gracie: "I was now working with the crew at the davits on the starboard side forward, adjusting them, ready for lowering the Engelhardt boat from the roof of the officers' house to the Boat Deck below. Some one of the crew on the roof, where it was, sang out, 'Has any passenger a knife?' I took mine out of my pocket and tossed it to him saying, "Here is a small penknife, if that will do any good'. It appeared to me then that there was more trouble than there ought to have been in removing the canvas cover and cutting the boat loose, and that some means should have been available for doing this without any delay. Meantime, four or five long oars were placed aslant against the walls of the officers' house to break the fall of the boat, which was pushed from the roof and slipped with a crash down on the Boat Deck, smashing several of the oars. About this time I recall that an officer on the roof of the house called down to the crew at this quarter, 'Are there any seamen down there among you?' "Aye, aye, sir', was the response, and quite a number left the Boat Deck to assist in what I supposed to have been the cutting loose of the other Engelhardt boat up there on the roof. The crew had thrown the Engelhardt boat to the deck, but I did not understand why they were so long about launching it, unless they were waiting to cut the other one loose and launch them both at the same time."

When collapsible A came crashing down onto the boat deck, people in the immediate area converged on it like bees to honey. The intent was to get it over to the same davits that were used to lower collapsible C a few minutes earlier. Everyone in the area was aware of two things. First, time was running out for launching more lifeboats. Second, if the crew succeeded in launching this boat, it would be the last chance to get off the ship. Murdoch and Moody were focused on the first problem -

getting the boat set up before the ship went under. The passengers in the area were focused on the second - their last chance to get off in a lifeboat. Together, these two situations met with volatile results.

Senator Smith: "Were there many people on the boat deck at that time?"

Samuel Hemming: "Yes, sir."

Smith: "How many?"

Hemming: "I could not tell you. A good many."

Smith: "Several hundred?"

Hemming: "No, sir. I should not think it would amount to several hundred. It amounted to just one or two."

Smith: "It amounted to one or two hundred?"

Hemming: "Yes, sir."

Smith: "Men and women?"

Hemming: "No, sir. There were no women."

The men had to literally drag collapsible A across the deck to the empty davits through throngs of passengers and crew standing about. Many were steerage passengers who had just arrived and found all the boats were gone except this one. It was painfully obvious to everyone that there were not enough seats in that collapsible for

The forward starboard side of the Boat Deck where collapsible C was lowered and where collapsible A was prepared for loading. (Olympic)

61

Archibald Gracie

Archibald Gracie was a historian and a writer who found himself in the middle of one of the greatest human tragedies to occur in his lifetime. Almost immediately after his rescue, he went on to write an excellent account of the disaster, particularly regarding the details associated with the lowering of each and every lifeboat. It is a surprise then to find his observations at odds with the majority of other survivors in one key area.

Gracie did not mention any disturbances on the starboard side, despite a number of other witnesses who described rushes on a lifeboat and even shots fired either at people or in the air. His accounts are so detailed, it is hard to imagine how he would have forgotten to mention skirmishes and guns being fired, for he places himself on both sides of the boat deck during these disturbances. Yet his lack of mention of any of these when a number of other survivors spoke of them raises a question concerning his accuracy. There are four possible explanations for his silence on this subject.

One possibility lies in his whereabouts those last twenty minutes. He was on the move continuously and when the disturbances occurred, he may have always been somewhere else. For instance, when the skirmish took place at collapsible C and a gun was fired, Gracie was perhaps helping with collapsible D on the port side. When the passengers rushed collapsible D and Lightholler used his gun, Gracie may already have followed orders and gone to the starboard side. When Murdoch later had trouble with passengers rushing collapsible A Gracie may have been over the port side assisting the women in getting into collapsible D just before it was lowered. Finally, when the last shots were fired near the starboard side of the bridge just before the plunge, Gracie may have been too far back in the crowd at that point to notice.

A second possibility for the differences from other passengers accounts may have been an attempt on Gracie's behalf to preserve the dignity of the officers. Gracie and Lightholler had spoken at length after the disaster on the rescue ship Carpathia, and it is possible the two may have informally agreed that it would be best to minimize any incidences of an officer firing his gun (although Gracie mentioned at the Senate inquiry that Lightholler told him he had fired a gun during the loading of collapsible D). In the case of Murdoch in particular, the two could have concluded that such talk would be a dishonor to the memory of a man who had just lost his life.

The third explanation for the discrepancy may stem from the fact that Gracie was a historian. He had just survived the most incredible maritime disaster. Perhaps it was too much for him to resist the temptation to embellish his experiences a little - placing himself alongside the crew loading the boats, later helping women to the last lifeboat, later still assisting in getting the collapsibles down from the officers quarters - when he may not have been in all the places he says he was.

The last possibility, is that Archibald Gracie's account is absolutely right, and the other witnesses who spoke of skirmishes at the lifeboats and shots fired were the ones embellishing.

Anything is possible, including a combination of all of the above. But it needs to be taken under consideration when reading Archibald Gracie's accounts. Gracie himself did not have the opportunity to answer questions about the details in his book. His health continued to decline after his amazing survival from the disaster. He died in December 1912 before his book was published.

Water accumulates at the forward end of C deck in a first class cabin area.

all the people there. A sort of survival-of-the-fittest panic began to set in. As Murdoch, Moody and other crew and passengers helped push the boat across the deck, people began jumping in to assure themselves a seat. Murdoch, exasperated with the chore of getting this boat launched under these circumstances, issued a warning to keep out of the boat.

But no sooner did they proceed than passengers pressed for the few seats, jumping into the boat again. Murdoch, fully understanding the seriousness of getting this boat launched quickly, and the number of additional lives it could save, could not tolerate the unfolding chaos. He snapped.

George Rheims: "While the last boat was leaving, I saw an officer with a revolver fire a shot and kill a man who was trying to climb into it."

Eugene Daly: "At the first cabin when a boat was being lowered an officer pointed a revolver and said if any man tried to get in, he would shoot him on the spot. I saw the officer shoot two men dead because they tried to get in the boat."

Both of these witnesses were picked up the following morning from collapsible A, proving they were in the immediate area to see the shooting. One of the unfortunate passengers who was likely involved in the scuffle was third class Edward Lindell from Sweden. In Gracie's book, a letter is quoted from Harold Wingate of the White Star Line in which he comments on the contents of collapsible A when found later by a passing liner: "There was also a ring found in the boat whose owner we eventually traced in Sweden and restored the property to her. We cannot account for its being in the boat, but we know that her husband was a passenger on the Titanic, Edward P. Lindell, a third class passenger." Since Lindell's body was not found in the boat, it is very probable that the ring came off during the scuffle on the Titanic's deck. In fact, Edward P. Lindell may have been shot in that boat. When shots rang out, passengers in the lifeboats thought they were hearing explosions.

Senator Fletcher: "Did you hear any explosions on the ship?"
John Hardy: "Yes sir, I fancied I did. There were two direct reports."
Fletcher: "What did it sound like, the giving way of bulkheads or the bursting of boilers?"
Hardy: "That I could not say. There were two reports or explosions. What it was, I do not know. I was not able to say."

Alfred Olliver: "I heard several little explosions, but it was not such explosions as I expected to hear. Before she sank and while she was sinking."

Smith: "Did you hear any explosions?"
Herbert Pitman: "Yes; four reports."
Smith: "What kind of reports?"
Pitman: "They sounded like the reports of a big gun in the distance."

Henry Stengel, a first class passenger knew where some of the shots came from based upon what he witnessed when he saw his wife off earlier in a starboard lifeboat.

Henry Stengel: "I saw two, a certain physician in New York and his brother, jump into the same boat my wife was in. Then the officer or the man that was loading the boat said 'I will stop that. I will go down and get my gun.' He left the deck momentarily and came right back again. Afterwards I heard about five shots; that is, while we were afloat."

Murdoch was in charge of loading the

boats on the starboard side and it is likely that he was the officer Stengel described.

By now, collapsible A had been positioned in the davits. But somewhere along the way the officers had changed their minds and dropped any further efforts to launch the boat. One clue to why collapsible A was abandoned by the officers lies with the sides of the collapsible. They were never put up into position. A couple of survivors mentioned working on the davits in order to prepare the boat for launching, but why were the sides never raised? The lifeboat had been damaged when it was dropped from the roof of the officers quarters. Besides the problem with the canvas sides, it is likely that once the crew reached the edge of the boat deck with the collapsible and saw how close the water was - less than ten feet away - they decided that hooking the boat up this late to the davits would almost certainly condemn it to go down with the ship. It was just about this time that Samuel Hemming arrived on the scene.

Samuel Hemming: "After I had finished with the lamps, when I made my last journey they were turning out the port collapsible boat. I went and assisted Mr. Lightoller to get it out. After the boat was out I went to the top of the officers' house and helped to clear away the port collapsible boat on that house. After that I went over to the starboard side. The starboard collapsible boat had just been lowered. I rendered up the foremast fall, got the block on board, and held on to the block while a man equalized the parts of the fall. He said, 'There is a futterfoot in the fall', which fouls the fall and the block. I says, 'I have got it', and took it out. I passed the block up to the officers' house, and Mr. Moody, the sixth officer said, 'We don't want the block. We will leave the boat on deck'. I put the fall on the deck, stayed there a moment, and there was no chance of the boat being cleared away, and I went to the bridge and looked over and saw the water climbing upon the bridge. I went over to the starboard side and everything was black. I went over to the port side and saw a boat off the port quarter, and I went along the port side and got up the after boat davits and slid down the fall and swam to the boat and got it."

It should be noted that when Hemming mentioned that everything on the starboard side was black, he was speaking of how there were no lifeboats visible in the darkness. When he crossed over to the port side, it was lifeboat number 4 that he saw, still floundering about near the side of the ship.

Mrs. Stephenson: "We implored the men to pull away from the ship but they refused, and we pulled three men into the boat who had dropped off the ship and were swimming towards us. One man was drunk and had a bottle of brandy in his pocket which the quartermaster promptly threw overboard and the drunken man was thrown into the bottom of the boat and a blanket thrown over him. After these three men were hauled in, they told how fast the ship was sinking and we all implored them to pull for our lives to get out from the suction when she should go down."

At this point the question must be asked. Where was Captain Smith? Lightoller does not mention him being present at this late time on the port side, and nobody makes mention of him on the starboard side either. It is a gallant thought to imagine him "on the bridge to the last", but realistically, there was nothing to be done there - not to mention that it was overrun by passengers and crew. It is likely that he was inside the officers quarters taking care of some personal business of which we will never know the specifics, perhaps collecting a photograph of his wife and daughter, rounding up his money, or making a final entry in the ships log.

Harold Bride related that Captain Smith poked his head into their wireless cabin right around this time to relieve them of their duties, further indicating that he was circulating about the officers quarters. Some may have engaged him in some final business and best wishes.

Lightoller: "The purser, as a matter of fact, both the pursers, and the pursers' assistants of whom I believe there were four, two pursers and four assistants, and two doctors were there. It was obvious to me that everything with regard to their duty had been done by the mere fact that shortly before the vessel sank, I met a purser, Mr. McElroy, Mr. Barker, Dr. O'Loughlin and Dr. Simpson and the four assistants. They were just coming from the direction of the bridge. They were evidently just keeping out of everybody's way. They were keeping away from the crowd so as not to interfere with the loading of the boats. McElroy, if I remember, was walking along with his hands in his pockets. The pursers assistant was coming behind with the ship's bag, showing that all detail work had been attended to . I think one of them had a roll of papers under his arm,

The third class General Room

showing that they had been attending to their detail work. That is why I draw the conclusion. They were perfectly quiet. They came up to me and just shook hands and said, "good bye, old man." We said good bye to each other and that is all there was to it."

With Captain Smith apparently absent on both sides of the deck, the pursers, who were basically the hotel managers of the Titanic, were probably with Captain Smith somewhere inside the officers quarters, going over final business with respect to the contents of the safes and other paperwork. Since it is unlikely that any of these men realized the extent of the icy water waiting for them, it would make perfect sense that they felt the need to go over some issues with Captain Smith before the vessel foundered. The fact that the contents of the safes were never loaded into a lifeboat implies that even the pursers may never have realized until too late that the Titanic was actually going to sink. Whatever they discussed with the captain, and whatever they were carrying with them will never be known since the captain, the pursers, their assistants, and the doctors were all lost. The bags and papers they were carrying went down with the ship.

Meanwhile, a number of passengers were still inside the ship at various locations. There were 1,500 people still on board, and at the most a couple hundred on the Boat Deck. The sheer number of this many people would not have fit into the stern poop deck. Many steerage passengers were sitting in the third class General Room and Smoking Room, which were located alongside each other under the poop deck. Because of the cold weather and the fact that this part of the ship was well above the waterline, these two rooms were probably very crowded with standing room only.

Some steerage passengers set off into the ship in search of an alternate way up to the lifeboats, not realizing how dangerously close the ship was to sinking. From the height of the stern above the water, they were easily mislead into thinking they still had plenty of time to walk through the ship. Little

did they know that the Titanic was not going to continue sinking at a measured pace, but was instead critically close to taking a plunge that would set in motion a rapid sinking of the liner.

Back on the port side of the boat deck, they were still working on getting the collapsible B down from the roof. The ropes were freed, and now several oars were lined up along the walls of the officers' quarters, just as they did with collapsible A on the starboard side. From the roof, it was painfully clear how close the water was to reaching the boat deck.

Having finished whatever unknown business he was involved with, Captain Smith returned one last time to the bridge. He could hear the skirmishes of the crowds on the starboard side. At the same time, the band was playing the ragtime tune "Autumn" on the port side. Looking through the forward windows, he could see the water just outside. It was an extraordinarily unusual sight for a man who had gazed out from many bridges during a long and successful career that spanned several decades. He had maneuvered ships through fog and storms on countless voyages across the Atlantic. Now, he was standing on the bridge of the largest ocean liner in the world and before him lay

not the proud bow of a ship defiantly cutting through the Atlantic water on a cold April night. Instead, just outside the window was the icy cold Atlantic lapping against the wall only a few feet below. The bridge - his bridge - was about to go under.

Captain Smith's mind must have been swirling like the water pouring into his ship. Many things must have crossed his mind at that point - the temperature of the water, the number of people left on board without lifeboats, the rescue ship Carpathia reporting that she was still two hours away, the mysterious ship sitting on the horizon. He knew that he had been warned of ice several times in the last couple days and that he was not on the bridge when his ship was traveling through the ice region. His mind must have dwelled on many emotional thoughts, including his wife and his daughter. This was his last voyage before retiring to spend more time with them. He had no intention of going under with his ship and made his move to get off the sinking liner.

Captain Smith left the bridge of the Titanic for the last time and walked outside onto the port wing. To his left, he could see some people standing on the boat deck looking up toward the roof of the officers quarters. He may have gallantly warned them one more time to "Abandon ship!", "Be British", or "It's every man for himself" but it is only speculation at this point. Using the outside wall to hoist himself up, he climbed on top of the forward railing and stood there for a moment, resting his hand on the roof of the bridge. The water immediately below him glowed an eerie green as a result of the submerged A and B deck lights. With no time to lose, he took a breath, and dove into the water. As would be experienced fifteen hundred times that night by fifteen hundred individuals, the icy cold water stabbed at Captain Smith as he entered, taking his breath away and causing his entire body to clinch tight. Harold Bride, standing on the roof while working to free collapsible B, had a birds eye view of the captain's departure from the foundering ship.

Bride: "The last I saw of the captain of the Titanic, he went overboard from the bridge about, I should think, three minutes before I left it myself."

The ship was still leaning over to the port side, although mildly now, so that there was less time available to launch collapsible B compared to starboard collapsible A. As the crew shoved the boat

up to the edge of the roof in preparation for pushing it over onto the boat deck, Lightoller decided there was no point in even climbing back down to the boat deck. From his vantage point, he must have seen the water swirling around the docking bridge and the forward railing.

The plan to lower collapsible B was the same as collapsible A - to be lowered to the boat deck by sliding it down along the oars posted at angles along the walls of the deck house. Seeing the water just about to come on deck, the crew hurried and quickly pushed the boat over the side with all their might. Something went awry in the rush, and the collapsible flipped over and landed upside down onto the boat deck with a crash.

Senator Smith: "How many people were in the boat or on the boat when it fell from the upper deck on to the lower deck?"
Harold Bride: "There was not anybody in it. It was pushed over intentionally."
Smith: "Was it fastened to the boat davits?"
Bride: "No, sir; it was resting on a proper bed there for it."
Smith: "How did you get in it?"
Bride: "When it was pushed over onto the A deck (Bride referred to the boat deck as "A deck"), we all scrambled down onto A deck

again."
Smith: "You all scrambled in?"
Bride: "We did not scramble in. We scrambled down onto A deck and were going to launch it properly."

From the lifeboats, passengers' eyes were glued to the ship. When the Titanic's running lights just below the bridge disappeared, many in the boats knew the end was near. The reality of the scene struck them. They were watching the Titanic sink, and she was starting to sink fast. The last lifeboats to leave were close enough to see the crowds gathering at the stern. They could see another group at the front of the boat deck, near the waterline. And they could see a few in between, some walking, some running, some just standing there.

The Titanic was still magnificent. Although her bow was now gone and she was significantly down by the head, the combination of the orchestra music drifting out over the water and all of her lights ablaze hypnotized all who watched. To those in the lifeboats, the great ship looked as though she was going to go out peacefully. As if to signal everyone that the Titanic was ready for the end, the band stopped playing and the ship went quiet. A chill went through many

A passenger watches the Titanic in her final peaceful minutes before the plunge.

watching from a distance. The tranquil scene before them would not last, as the Titanic was about to go into a violent death throe before their eyes.

As the band put down their instruments, the water came over the steel half wall along the port side bridge and poured onto the deck. The group disbanded and whatever happened to them from that moment onward is unknown.

The roar of the releasing steam from the funnels had stopped some time ago and the forward slant, although significant, was not yet steep enough for everything moveable to start sliding forward. There was an occasional crash here and there from within, but for the most part, the Titanic was quiet for just a moment. On the port side, the only sound was that of the water sliding onto the boat deck. It was the calm before the storm.

Where Did They Come From?

One of the more interesting - and disturbing - observations made by Archibald Gracie in his 1912 book titled "The Truth About the Titanic" was the following, made when the water was racing up the boat deck:

"We had taken but a few steps in the direction indicated when there arose before us from the decks below, a mass of humanity several lines deep, covering the Boat Deck, facing us, and completely blocking our passage toward the stern. There were women in the crowd, as well as men, and they seemed to be steerage passengers who had just come up from the decks below."

Where were these passengers coming from just moments before the ship sank? Most steerage passengers climbed the outside deck ladders or took the main staircase in second class up to the boat deck toward the stern of the ship. But why were these people coming up the forward Grand Staircase when there were a number of faster and safer ways to get up to the boat deck? And why were they arriving so late, when other third class passengers, including men, had arrived in the area as early as fifteen minutes sooner? Only seconds after these passengers came out of the Grand Staircase doorway, it was sealed off by the rising water.

Archibald Gracie was standing by the entranceway to the first class Grand Staircase on the starboard side. The same deck on the port side was going underwater because of the lean to port so it is doubtful they were crossing over from that side.

The fact that they were traveling in

The gymnasium windows. Next to the doorway in the distance is the entrance to the Grand Staircase where many steerage passengers appeared only moments before the ship sank. (Olympic)

such a large group eliminates the possibility they climbed any outside deck ladders, since this is a one-by-one process and would have considerably slowed down a group of this size. They must have traveled by established staircases and there were only two main staircases on the Titanic that lead from the lower decks straight up to the boat deck. One was the Grand Staircase, and the other was the second class main staircase. The Grand Staircase down on E deck was completely submerged, and on D deck partially flooded. By contrast, the second class main staircase nearer the stern also went up to the boat deck and was completely dry. By all accounts, these passengers should have passed by the second class main staircase first - and should have taken it to the boat deck. But for some unknown reason, they went by it and instead, dangerously ended up on the Grand Staircase only moments before it went under water.

How did they come to be there? A study of the Titanic's deck plans reveals two possible ways. They either started from the open well on C deck and traveled the upper decks of second and first class, or they set off toward the bow all the way down on E deck.

If the group had traveled the upper decks from the well deck, something must

The main stairway in second class. A key artery to the boat deck, it was bypassed for some unknown reason by many third class passengers as they searched for a passage to the lifeboats.

have drawn them forward to walk right by the second class main staircase - something like an open door leading into the first class Cafe Parisien on B deck, or into the hallway of first class cabins on C deck. Perhaps, even at this dire time, these steerage passengers were just a little bit curious to see first class. Entering the first class areas on either of these two decks would have quickly lead them to the first class rear staircase which went as high as A deck. Unlike the second class staircase, which was behind a set of doors, this first class staircase on both B and C decks was very obvious. They could not possibly have missed it and had they used this set of stairs, they would have come out

The entranceway to the Grand Staircase on the Promenade Deck (Olympic)

before it went under.

If these steerage passengers had set off for the bow from below on E deck, it may have been driven by a particular condition that night in third class - a shortage of real estate. There were scores of steerage passengers roused out of their cabins and assembled in the public areas. Anyone who has been to sporting event, concert or any large gathering knows how chaotic crowds can be when they are standing about. Imagine hundreds and hundreds of people milling about the third class poop deck, stairwell, and inside the narrow passageways on D and E decks and then add to this picture the crew telling them to stay there for about two hours. This is a very long time to be standing around in a crowd. It is easy to see how families and groups of friends, particularly those that were backed up all the way down to D and E decks, could decide there had to be a better course of action than standing around in the hallways and stairwells with hundreds of other people while the slant of the deck grew. It was a scenario like this that would have given birth to groups of people setting off deep into the ship to find their way to the boat deck.

Their route at this late hour must have been extremely interesting. After four days at

onto the A deck promenade. From there they would have headed down the slant of the deck until they reached the A deck entrance to the Grand Staircase. However, there are two problems with this scenario. First, there was a staircase midway on the Promenade Deck they could not have missed that went up to the boat deck. Second, the forward Promenade Deck was flooded by now and the A deck entrance by this time had to be perilously close to going under water. It is hard to conceive that these passengers would have raced down the decks to the rising water, only to duck inside a doorway seconds sea, they would have explored the third class areas of the ship by now. They were very familiar with "Scotland Road" down on E deck and knew that it traveled the length of the ship. They also knew there were many doors along that corridor that lead to other areas. One of them, they must have thought, would lead them to the boat deck. Heading down the slant of E deck from their own main staircase aft, they passed through the first open watertight door (these doors were opened at the rear of the ship to allow third class passengers and crew to move about). On the right hand side was a doorway that lead to one of the second class main stairways. Another 75 feet through a second watertight doorway would have lead them past yet another second class stairway. Both of these went to the upper decks in second class, and the latter went all the way to the boat deck. Why they did not choose these stairs here is equally as mysterious as why they did not choose them under the other scenario. If they were searching for a way to the boat deck, it is hard to believe they overlooked these staircases. Survivors mentioned that the doors to these staircases were open. Is it possible they were later locked? Perhaps there were crew posted somewhere on these staircases to prevent

Steerage passengers likely passed through the first class dining room only minutes before the ship began its final plunge. (Olympic)

steerage passengers from using them, just as crew were posted at the top of the open well deck stairs. It is a mystery why, but it is a fact all the same that this group did not use these stairs.

Continuing down E deck, they would have searched for staircases that lead up to higher decks. Initially, they found several that instead went down to F deck. Rounding a corner, they reached Scotland Road, complete with its forward view of much of the ship's length. However, by this late hour, the view was a considerably short one. The water was only seventy feet ahead, pouring down the staircase into the third class dining saloon on F deck. The E deck corridor gradually disappeared beneath the ominous green surface. Their course would have been at a dead end, except for one particular door just across the hallway from where they stood. Opening it, they climbed a narrow staircase that went up one flight to D deck.

At the top of the steps they found themselves in the first class pantry. Had they traveled around the corner to the back side of the stairs, they would have found a door to yet another narrow flight of stairs that eventually lead all the way up to the boat deck farther aft of the Grand Staircase. Instead, they walked through the swinging doors nearby that opened into the first class dining room. There was little time to take in much of the room, but they must have glanced about them as they walked downhill along the carpeted floors and set tables. Passing through the doorway at the other end, they came to the Reception Room. At the base of the stairs they were greeted by the water, temporarily stopped while the flooding third class dining rooms below siphoned off any advancing water. They walked cautiously, but quickly through it and hurried up the steps. On the way, they could not have helped but notice the wrought iron railings with gold leaf highlights.

By now, the ship was only seconds from beginning her final plunge. Somewhere around A deck, the ship lurched forward, and they hurried their ascent until finally reaching the boat deck. Running out onto the deck, it was too late for them. To their surprise, not only were there no remaining lifeboats, but they found they had just missed being trapped inside the ship by advancing water.

We will never know for sure where these passengers came from. Their desperate appearance at the Grand Staircase implies there is much that we still do not know about the treatment of the third class passengers.

The Titanic looked terminal. The sea was right up to the bridge and any hope that the ship was somehow going to stay afloat no longer seemed possible. Deep within, the water overtook the third class dining rooms and made headway again along the other decks. It traveled up the C deck hallway, stealing quietly under the door of each stateroom without knocking. It continued its creep along the carpeting of the Reception Room on D deck. It searched along the E deck hallway for the stairwell leading down to the next watertight compartment. Further below, boiler room number 4 was still flooding, but not fast enough to offset the immense pressure mounting all around. Three decks of water bore down on the compartment from within the ship while it felt the squeeze from outside - now eight stories below sea level. The forward bulkhead of boiler room number 4 was the front line in keeping the Titanic buoyant, bearing the weight of the 45,000 ton liner as she slanted forward into the ocean.

Closer to the bow, water leaked into the vessel through the submerged cargo hatch covers. They were designed to protect the ship from flooding under heavy seas and were doing a good job so far in holding back the inevitable. Had an area the size of those hatches been open to the sea once the bow dipped under, the ship would never have lasted twenty minutes.

Joseph Boxhall: "There is a watertight cover just to prevent the sea going down. There are wooden hatches on the top beams instead of the coamings; wooden hatches laid across the beams, and after the hatches are put on, the watertight covers are spread over".

These hatches, however were now under 30 to 40 feet of water and pressure was steadily building on them. Clearly, they would have a breaking point, and that moment was about to arrive. Between the immense pressure on boiler room 4 and the mounting pressure on the cargo hatch covers, a catastrophic failure in the buoyancy of the ship was about to occur. There was a time bomb of sorts deep within the Titanic and it was about to go off.

The scene on the forward boat deck was deteriorating into pure chaos. Collapsible A was lined up with the empty davits but not attached, and crowds climbed into it and pressed around the boat as it sat on deck. As noted earlier by Hardy, Officer Moody already took a position that the boat was not going to be lowered along the side, and it appears the senior officers wrote collapsible A off as unlaunchable. The area was so filled with people that if anyone standing near the collapsible wanted to leave, they could not do so easily considering the numbers pressing forward. Many made the decision not to go near the boat and stayed back by the gymnasium and Grand Staircase entranceway.

Over on the port side, things were at a final desperate point. Because of the Titanic's lean in that direction, the forward end of the port boat deck was sliding under the water. Collapsible B sat upside down on the deck for a brief moment while the crew and some passengers approached it. Within seconds, water swirled around the overturned collapsible, picked it up, and carried it away from the deck.

Smith: "Then what happened?"
Bride: "It was washed overboard before we had time to launch it."

By 2:15 the F deck third class dining rooms were submerged and water was advancing again up D and E decks. The weight of all this water surrounding the remaining boiler rooms was enormous, setting the stage for the sudden final plunge of the Titanic.

Smith: *"You then went down with it?"*
Bride: *"I happened to be nearest it and I grabbed it."*
Smith *"Did anyone else grab it?"*
Bride: *"No, sir."*
Smith: *"You went down with it alone?"*
Bride: *"Yes sir."*

Lightoller, in the meantime had walked around the base of the first funnel to the starboard side of the officers roof. There he saw Murdoch still by the last lifeboat.

Lightoller: *"He (Murdoch) was getting the boats out on the starboard side later on."*
Senator Smith: *"Did you see him at work?"*
Lightoller: *"No sir; I was on the port side".*
Smith: *"How do you know that he did it?"*
Lightoller: *"I saw him at the last boat."*

Lightoller worked the port side lifeboats right up to when he climbed onto the officers' quarters to push collapsible B down. It was from the roof that he would have seen over to the starboard side of the boat deck where Murdoch was working. His observation is an important one for two reasons. First, it locates Murdoch at collapsible A on the starboard side seconds before the ship's plunge. Second, it locates Lightoller on the starboard side of the roof seconds before the plunge. Collapsible A was already down on the boat deck. Why was Lightoller over on the starboard side roof now when there was critical work to be done in getting collapsible B off the port side roof? He went up on the roof for the very purpose of unlashing the lifeboat and getting it down, but for some reason he did not follow through with it's launching, as evidenced by Bride's and then Lightoller's own testimony.

Bride: "I went to the place I had seen the collapsible boat on the boat deck, and to my surprise I saw the boat and the men still trying to push it off. I guess there wasn't a sailor in the crowd. They couldn't do it."

Lightoller: "I understand the men standing on top, who assisted to launch it down, jumped onto it as it was on the deck and floated off with it."

What would have caused Lightoller to stop assisting with the port side collapsible on the roof, with so little time left, and instead walk around the funnel to the starboard side where there was no work to be done? Something drew Lightoller over to the starboard side.

By now, the water was gurgling just a few feet from where Officer Murdoch stood near the top of the stairway that lead up from the Promenade Deck. Before him stood a crowd in and around Collapsible A, with more steerage passengers arriving every moment. He must have felt responsible for what was unfolding before him. The brand new Titanic, the largest ocean liner in the world, was sinking into the dark, icy cold Atlantic with scores of people still on board - and all because of a collision with an iceberg that occurred while he was in charge of the bridge. Murdoch fired the gun earlier, so it felt familiar in his hand now. If he really had gone so far as to shoot one or two men attempting to get into the lifeboat earlier, he may have felt fatalistic at this point. Seeing the water so near now, it was the perfect time for someone considering suicide to go through with it. In the midst of the crowd, did Murdoch lift the gun to his head and fire?

Eugene Daly: " ... Afterwards there was another shot, and I saw the officer himself lying on the deck. They told me he shot himself, but I did not see him."

George Rheims: "As there remained nothing more for him to do, the officer told us, 'Gentlemen, each man for himself, Good bye'. He gave a military salute and then fired a bullet into his head. That's what I call a man!"

A person's view in that area of the boat deck would have been very limited, blocked by heads and shoulders of the crowd. Add to that the glare of the deckhouse lights and the contrast of the dark shadows cast by all the people, and a person would have actually been able to see very little.

John Collins: "There were hundreds on the starboard side."

Under these conditions, only those nearby, and only those who happened to be looking in Murdoch's direction would have witnessed the ghastly scene. Most people would have heard the shot and simply not known what it was. Again, many in the nearby boats thought they were hearing explosions of some sort.

Alfred Crawford: "I heard an explosion when we were lying to in the water, in the boat. Sort of a sharp, like as if there were things being blown up."

Major Peuchen: "I heard the explosions. A sort of rumbling sound. It was not a sharp sound - more of a rumbling kind of a sound, but still sharp at the same time. It would not be as loud as a clap of thunder or anything that way, or like a boiler explosion, I should not think. I should think they were from above (the water). I am not absolutely certain of this, because there was a good deal of excitement at the time, but I imagine there were three, one following the other very quickly."

Lowe: "I heard explosions, yes. I should say about four."

There were already several scuffles on the ship and this was not the first time shots were fired. Even though several survivors were on the starboard side of the boat deck up to the end, such a critical event may not have registered with them because of the crowds. They may simply not have been close enough to see it. Those who could have seen evidence of a suicide, like Rheims and Daly, went on to tell their story. Most in the area close enough to see something did not survive. The sound of the

gun shot might have been remembered more accurately by the rest of the survivors had it been an isolated event. But it was not. It would quickly take a back seat to what immediately followed. If there was more time, many would have asked "What was that?" Word would have spread through the crowd with some even forcing their way forward to see for themselves. But there was no time for such inquiries. From that moment on, each passenger was in a fight for their life. No sooner had the shots rung out than the final plunge of the Titanic began.

William Ward: "She gave a kind of sudden lurch forward, and I heard a couple of reports, reports more like a volley of musketry than anything else. You would not exactly call them a heavy explosion. It did not seem to me like an explosion at all."

Henry Stengel: "... and all of a sudden there were four sharp explosions about that far apart, just like this (indicated by snapping his fingers four times), and then she dipped ..."

Carl Jansen: "Suddenly I heard shrieks and cries amidship, and the sharp reports of several shots. People began to run by me

toward the stern of the ship, and as I started to run I realized that the boat was beginning to go down very rapidly ..."*

Deep within the ship, the bulkhead of boiler room 4 took all the pressure it could stand. The compartment gave way, and it gave way completely and all at once, setting off a chain reaction throughout the ship. With the loss of buoyancy at that location, the Titanic took a plunge forward, creating a surge of increased pressure on many areas of the submerged bow, including the forward hatches. The plunge was almost like a giant punch to the hatch covers. Already under extreme pressure, they too collapsed, giving way to an inflow of water greater than the damage created by the iceberg.

On the boat deck, nobody saw the plunge coming. When it happened, it created the equivalent of a small tidal wave that pounced on the deck so abruptly and without warning that it immediately engulfed the crowd gathered around collapsible A. No one in that area had time to react and anyone in the collapsible was washed off, as the lifeboat itself became temporarily immersed. Last seen standing by the officers quarters, Sixth Officer Moody was inundated by the rush of water. Chief Officer Wilde's whereabouts were unknown. Keeping in mind that the captain had released the crew from duty only minutes earlier, he may have been caught inside his quarters rounding up some of his personal belongings.

Lightoller: "Just then the ship took a slight but definite plunge - probably a bulkhead went - and the sea came rolling up in a wave, over the steel fronted bridge, along the deck below us, washing the people back in a dreadful huddled mass. Those that didn't disappear under the water right away, instinctively started to clamber up that part of the deck still out of water, and work their way towards the stern, which was rising steadily out of the water as the bow went down. It was a sight that doesn't bear dwelling on - to stand there, above the wheelhouse, and on our quarters, watching the frantic struggles to climb up the sloping deck, utterly unable to even hold out a helping hand."

A. Weikman: "I was proceeding to launch the next boat when the ship suddenly sank at the bow and there was a rush of water that washed me overboard, and therefore the boat was not launched by human hands. The men were trying to pull up the sides when the rush

of water came, and that was the last moment it was possible to launch any more boats, because the ship was at an angle that it was impossible for anybody to remain on deck."

John Collins: "I ran back to the deck, ran to the port side on the saloon deck with another steward and a woman and two children, and the steward had one of the children in his arms and the woman was crying. I took the child off of the woman and made for one of the boats. Then the word came around from the starboard side there was a collapsible boat getting launched on the starboard side and that all women and children were to make for it. So me and another steward and the two children and the woman came around on that side, the starboard side, and when we got around there we saw that it was forward. We saw the collapsible boat taken off of the saloon deck, and then the sailors and the firemen that were forward seen the ship's bow in the water and seen that she was intending to sink her bow, and they shouted out for all they were worth we were to go aft, and word came there was a boat getting launched, so we were to go aft, and we were just turning around and making for the stern end when the wave washed us off the deck - washed us clear of it - and the

child was washed out of my arms and the wreckage and the people that was around me, they kept me down for at least two or three minutes under the water."

The wave was approximately the height of a person and crashed over the bridge and side gunwale. The volume of water closing in on the boat deck was immense and immediate. To those it did not instantly submerge, the wave smashed into them, knocking them over and under while throwing others against the boat deck wall. The ship not only plunged downward, but seemed to move forward, creating a suction and numerous whirlpools about the area for those caught in the wake to grapple with. For the first time that night, large numbers of people were now in the icy cold Atlantic.

The water continued up the deck, roaring after the remaining crowd. Those further back sprang into action and ran for the stern with the wave fast at their heels.

Gracie: " ... Clinch Smith made the proposition that we should leave and go toward the stern, still on the starboard side, so he started and I followed immediately after him. We had taken but a few steps in the direction indicated when there arose before

Third class passengers retreat from the wave racing up the boat deck.

us from the decks below, a mass of humanity several lines deep, covering the boat deck, facing us, and completely blocking our passage toward the stern. There were women in the crowd, as well as men, and they seemed to be steerage passengers who had just come up from the decks below. Instantly,

when they saw us and the water on the deck chasing us from behind, they turned in the opposite direction towards the stern. This brought them at that point plumb against the iron fence and railing which divide the first and second class passengers. Even among these people there was no hysterical cry, or

evidence of panic, but oh, the agony of it!"

It is incredible to think that steerage passengers were coming up the Grand Staircase in first class this late - just moments before the water blocked off the exitway on the boat deck. Prior to the plunge, the ship was taking in water at a good clip, but the Titanic still felt solid under one's feet. The water was all the way down around the D deck landing as they climbed the final flight of stairs to the boat deck. As they hurriedly passed the intricately carved paneling, the gold leaf wrought iron railing, and the clock surrounded by two statues representing "Honor and Glory Crowning Time", the ship took its plunge. The drop was noticeable and the sound it created was like a muffled, distant explosion. Water began splashing down through the bannister on the left from above. Reaching the boat deck foyer, they saw the water pour in through the port entranceway and rush down the nearby hallway forward. Instinctively they headed up the slant of the deck for the starboard exit. At the door, the large group bottle necked as they filed out one or two at a time. Those toward the back of this crowd were temporarily stopped. Prior to this, the ship had been eerily quiet inside. But now that the Titanic had started her final plunge, those at the back of the crowd could hear water roaring and gurgling down the staircase inside the ship as large volumes of it flowed in through the A deck entrance ways below. Things were starting to slide off tables and shelves now, and the sound of thuds and breaking glass were beginning to emanate throughout the ship. Imagine being at the back of that crowd in the Grand

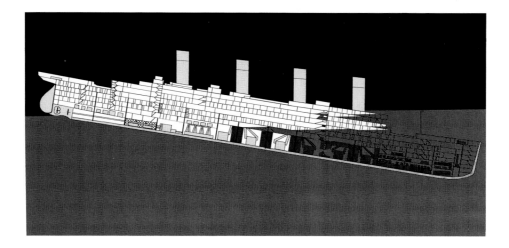

Staircase Foyer on boat deck, waiting to get through the door to the open deck! Gracie's observation that there was no hysterical cry or evidence of panic among them is nothing less than amazing.

Once outside, these passengers did not know where they were on the ship. They walked right into the middle of passengers who were rushing away from the approaching water. Not knowing what was going on, it is likely they just stood there attempting to get their wits about them, creating a human traffic jam. One look to their left and they would have seen the approaching wave. Now, these steerage passengers, who had traveled their odd and poorly timed route from the stern, turned and headed right back there again.

On the port side, collapsible B was already floating in the water when the ship took the plunge. The effect, however, threw the boat forward out ahead of the ship, spinning it around in the turbulent water swirling about the dying liner. Harold Bride was holding onto the upside down boat when the plunge began and the resulting wave washed everyone off the collapsible. Bride was tossed about but somehow managed to hold on.

Bride: "The big wave carried the boat off. I had hold of an oarlock and I went off with it. The next thing I knew I was in the boat. But that was not all. I was in the boat, and the boat was upside down, and I was under it. And I remember realizing that I was wet

A passenger on the Promenade Deck is caught off guard by the sudden dip of the ship and attempts to stay ahead of the inrush of water.

through, and that whatever happened I must not breathe, for I was under water. I know I had to fight for it, and I did. How I got out from under the boat I do not know, but I felt a breath of air at last."

Bride lost sight of collapsible B as it swirled away ahead of the first funnel and over a bit toward the starboard side. There were hundreds of people in the water at this point, and several quickly grabbed hold of the overturned boat as it floated by, some even climbing up on it. Oddly enough, collapsible A, which was washed overboard from the starboard side boat deck, also went cascading forward with the suction of the ship, floated over the now submerged bridge, bumped up against the forward funnel, and spun around to the port side. Both collapsibles had effectively criss-crossed each other. Collapsible B was out ahead of the ship, collapsible A seemed to be stuck near her decks from the ongoing suction.

The wave was not high enough to wash over the roof of the officer's quarters, at least not where Lightoller was standing. However, when the plunge occurred, the bridge dropped beneath the surface and in an instant the water was washing along the roof and foaming towards Lightoller.

Lightoller: "It came to me very clearly how fatal it would be to get amongst those hundreds and hundreds of people who would shortly be struggling for their lives in that deadly cold water. There was only one thing to do, and I might just as well do it and get it over, so, turning to the fore part of the bridge, I took a header. Striking the water was like a thousand knives being driven into one's body, and for a few moments, I completely lost grip of myself - and no wonder for I was perspiring freely, whilst the temperature of the water was 28 degrees. Ahead of me the lookout cage on the foremast was visible just above the water - in normal times it would be a hundred feet above. I struck out blindly for this, but only for a short while, till I got hold of myself again and realized the futility of seeking safety on anything connected with the ship."

Certain observations made by the survivors are invaluable and this is one of them. Lightoller's mention that the crow's nest was level with the water after the bridge dipped under establishes approximately how the Titanic sat in the water at this point. The stern had risen above the surface, but was not yet dangling. This emphasizes the sheer weight of the liner. It would take a considerable amount of water in the bow and an extreme angle to finally start pulling the stern clear out of the water. Both of these conditions were beginning to occur. Water was pouring into the front of the ship so quickly that there was no time for it to make its way to the rear of the ship. As a result, the ship began to take its infamous swan dive.

Lightoller attempted to swim from the ship but was quickly dragged back and pinned against a ventilation grate that stood just in front at the base of the first funnel and went all the way down to Boiler Room 6. As the ventilation fan sank below the surface, so too did Lightoller with it. By lucky timing, a burst of hot air came flying up from below and shot him to the surface. This is interesting because boiler room 6 should have been completely under water long ago. Where exactly did this large burst of air come from? Lightoller seemed to think it was the boilers exploding. Whatever the source, it pushed him away from the grating so that he came back to the surface. But before he could swim, he was immediately drawn up against yet another grate. Dazed and battered at this point, he could not recall how he got loose from it, but eventually came back to the surface, this time right next to the overturned collapsible B.

Lightoller: "There were many around in the water by this time, some swimming, others (mostly men, thank God), definitely drowning - an utter nightmare of both sight and sound."

Bride: "There were men all around me - hundreds of them. The sea was dotted with them, all depending on their lifebelts. I felt I simply had to get away from the ship. She was a beautiful sight then."

The wave created by the plunge quickly spent itself out on the deck so that as it washed along the end of the officers quarters it was waist high. As it proceeded up the deck, it foamed and tumbled forward, just as a wave does when it finishes up on the beach. By the time it reached Archibald Gracie's location it was much reduced, but still advancing, as the Titanic continued to sink by the bow.

Gracie: "Clinch Smith and I instantly saw that we could make no progress ahead, and with the water following us behind over the deck, we were in a desperate place. I can never forget the exact point on the ship where he and I were located, viz., at the opening of the angle made by the walls of the officer's house and only a short distance abaft the Titanic's forward expansion joint. Clinch Smith was immediately on my left, nearer the apex of the angle, and our backs were turned toward the ship's rail, and the sea. Looking up toward the roof of the officer's house I saw a man to the right of me and above lying on his stomach on the roof, with his legs dangling over. Clinch Smith jumped to reach this roof, and I promptly followed. The efforts of both of us failed. I was loaded down with heavy long-skirted overcoat and Norfolk coat beneath, with clumsy life-preserver over all, which made my jump fall short. As I came down, the water struck my right side. I crouched down into it preparatory to jumping with it, and rose as if on the crest of a wave on the seashore. This expedient brought the attainment of the object I had in view. I was able to reach the roof and the iron railing that is along the edge of it, and pulled myself over on top of the officer's house on my stomach near the base of the second funnel.

The feat which I instinctively accomplished was the simple one, familiar to all bathers in the surf at the seashore.. I had no time to advise Clinch Smith to adopt it. To my utter dismay, a hasty glance to my left and right showed that he had not followed my example, and that the wave, if I may call it such, which had mounted me to the roof, had completely covered him, as well as all people on both sides of me, including the man I had first seen athwart the roof. I was thus parted forever from my friend, Clinch Smith, with whom I had agreed to remain to the last struggle."

Clinch Smith was probably pulled under the water more so by the suction of the ship than what was left of the wave at that point. It emphasizes the dangerous condition of the water around that area. The water continued up the boat deck and swirled by the entranceway to the Grand Staircase, pouring in through the open foyer door across the black and white linoleum.

*Senator Smith: "Were there lights about the deck where the boats were being loaded?"
Etches: "Yes sir. The cabin doors and all were open, giving a good light there."*

Most of the water rushing through the open foyer door tumbled down the slant of the deck to a hallway leading forward to a few first class cabins, the wireless office, and the officers quarters. It was met halfway down the hall by water racing upwards, pouring in through the submerged bridge. The rest of the water cascaded across the linoleum and poured down the Grand Staircase. Water was already pouring in from the Promenade Deck below, and this only added to the volume flowing into the forward end of the ship.

Jack Thayer and Milton Long were standing near the railing just outside the gymnasium door. They watched the water surging up the deck, chasing after the crowd running aft. Both saw no point in heading for the stern after they watched passengers pile up at the gate that divided first class from the engineers section of the boat deck. Once over that gate, only ten or so yards ahead lay yet another gate which separated the second class section of the boat deck. As a result, many passengers were stuck in a crowd that could not get by these obstacles fast enough.

Jack Thayer: "As the water gained headway along the deck, the crowd gradually moved with it, always pushing toward the floating stern and keeping in from the rail of the ship as far as they could. We were a mass of hopeless, dazed humanity, attempting as the Almighty and Nature made us, to keep our final breath until the last possible moment. Occasionally, there had been a muffled thud or deadened explosion within the ship. Now, without warning, she seemed to start forward, moving forward and into the water at an angle of about fifteen degrees. This movement, with the water rushing up toward us was accompanied by a rumbling roar, mixed with more muffled explosions ... (Milton) Long and I had been standing by the starboard rail, about abreast of the second funnel. Our main thought was to keep away from the crowd and the suction. At the rail we were entirely free of the crowd. We had previously decided to jump into the water before she actually went down, so that we might swim some distance away, and avoid what we thought would be terrific suction. We had no time to think now, only to act. We shook hands, wished each other luck. I said 'Go ahead, I'll be right with you'. I threw my overcoat off as he climbed over the rail, sliding down facing the ship. Ten seconds later I sat on the rail. I faced out, and with a push of my arms and hands, jumped into the water as far out from the ship as I could.

When we jumped we were only twelve or fifteen feet above the water. I never saw Long again. His body was later recovered. I am afraid that the few seconds elapsing between our going, meant the difference between being sucked into the deck below, as I believe he was, or pushed out and then sucked down."

While the bow of the Titanic sank, it drew in so much water through the open windows, doors, and ventilation shafts that many people were sucked down and into the ship. The Titanic claimed the first of her victims. Some never came back to the surface, while others were held down so long that by the time they came back up it was too late. Others still, like Lightoller, Gracie, and Thayer were drawn under the water and through sheer will power held their breath and struggled back to the surface alive. They lived to tell their stories, but there were countless others experiencing the same thing at that moment. The water in the area immediately in front of the submerged ship at this time must have been frightful to swim in. The combination of giant bursts of air rising to the surface, pockets of water being sucked into the ship, and many swirling whirlpools created something similar to a

As scores of passengers bottleneck on deck in an attempt to scramble from the water, Milton Long drops along the side of the ship while Jack Thayer climbs the railing in preparation of his own jump. To the right, Archibald Gracie crouches to ride the swell of water while Clinch Smith tries to jump to the roof.

boiling pot - except this water was not boiling, it was deadly cold.

Scattered about were scores of people trying to stay alive now. Only three hours ago, most of these people were sound asleep in warm beds. Now they were floating in the Atlantic Ocean in the middle of the night in water so cold that it took their breath away on contact. Fighting cramps from the icy water and trying to regain their breath, many could not cry out and instead thrashed about as their bodies flooded with adrenaline and set them in the panic mode. Among this crowd was one of the richest men in the world, John Jacob Astor, from the same family of the Waldorf Astoria Hotel. He remained at the forward end of the boat deck when all the lifeboats left, and was near the crowd around Collapsible A before it was washed off. The wave caught him too and he found himself thrashing about in the frigid water ahead of the sinking ship. He spotted the overturned collapsible and swam for it.

Even under these circumstances, most in the water had their eyes glued to the flailing liner. From the front, her slanting lines were exaggerated and all of her decks were exposed and tilted downward. Before them, they watched the Titanic plunging, her lights still burning and hundreds of her passengers and crew clambering up the deck for the highest points on the stern. There was a foamy mist about her at the waterline. All the while, a continuous sound of banging and crashing came from within, along with the ship's structure moaning and hissing from the strain of the increasing tilt.

Lawrence Beesley: "It was partly a roar, partly a groan, partly a rattle, and partly a smash, and it was not a sudden roar as an explosion would be; it went on successively for some seconds, possibly fifteen to twenty ... But it was a noise no one had heard before, and no one wishes to hear again; it was stupefying, stupendous, as it came to us along the water. It was as if all the heavy things one could think of had been thrown downstairs from the top of a house, smashing each other and the stairs and everything in the way."

Jack Thayer: "It was like standing under a steel railway bridge while an express train passes overhead, mingled with the noise of a pressed steel factory and wholesale breakage of china."

Many at this time caught sight of the upside down collapsible and began to swim toward it. Although it was no better than a raft at this point, it's white bottom drew the men to it like moths to a flame. One or two had already climbed on its back while dozens of others arrived at its edge. Behind them, something extraordinary began to happen.

The stern began to lift out of the water - an area of ship approximately the length of a football field, except this was no football field. It was eleven stories high and made of steel, containing massive engines, miscellaneous furnishings, and over 1,000 people. This much weight rising out of the water created a terrible strain on the Titanic which was first felt on the upper decks as the ship tried to bend itself back down into the water. There were two expansion joints on the upper decks of the ship which were designed to move a little to alleviate the stress that an ocean liner typically experiences while at sea. When the stern began to lift out of the water, the expansion joint toward the front of the ship expanded - considerably. Unfortunately, two of the twelve cables which held the forward funnel in place crossed over this joint, and were attached to the boat deck behind it. Because of the tilt, the funnels were leaning forward. The two cables stretched as far as they could, then snapped. The cable on the port side of

the ship snapped first, and the funnel began to lean to starboard. A moment later, the starboard cable snapped.

Suddenly, the smokestack broke from its mounting and fell forward toward the water. As it broke free from the ship, the vibration knocked glowing red hot coal embers and soot into the air. When the water rushed in at the base, the air rushed out the top, spraying sparks into the night sky like a brief fireworks display.

Charlotte Collyer: " ... millions of sparks shot up to the sky, like rockets in a park on the night of a summer holiday. This red spurt

As hundreds rush for the stern, the forward smokestack breaks loose and crashes into the water, spewing sparks and coal soot into the air.

The immense size of the funnel was enough to crush those in its path when it fell into the water.

was fan shaped as it went up, but the sparks descended in every direction, in the shape of a fountain of fire."

Bride: "Smoke and sparks were rushing out of her funnel. There must have been an explosion, but we had heard none. We only saw the big stream of sparks."

In the water, the men heard the screeching and twisting of the steel as the funnel broke loose from its mounting. Those directly in its path watched the funnel for a brief moment with wonder as the sparks flew into the air, then suddenly realized that the funnel was coming down at them. It crashed into the water, crushing numerous people who had the bad luck to be in its path. Most were swimming for collapsible B and were just about to reach it when this finger of fate came down on them. Included in the unfortunate group was John Jacob Astor. His body was later picked up, mangled and covered with soot. The funnel missed the overturned collapsible by only a foot or so and the gigantic splash threw the capsized lifeboat even further away from the turbulent waters around the ship, knocking people off it a second time in the process.

As the bow of the Titanic plunged downward and the stern rose up, the ship began to rotate in place. This was possibly the lingering effect of the ship's persistent lean to port. As the open decks on the left side of the ship dipped under the water, they virtually grabbed the water into it. In the meantime, the water flowing into the openings on the starboard side fell down a slope inside the ship. This created a push motion. As a result, shortly after the disastrous crash of the forward funnel, the Titanic started to turn away, having thrown the funnel as a parting gift to those in the water.

Bride: "The ship was gradually turning on her nose - just like a duck does that goes down for a dive. I had only one thing on my mind - to get away from the suction."

In the first class smoking lounge, the room was no longer occupied just by first class gentlemen. Men had arrived from all over the ship and they were standing around drinking from the bar. There was a good

The first class smoking room windows. Many rushed by them as the ship was going under. (Olympic)

This was the deck layout awaiting the scores arriving at the Boat Deck railing aft. Promenade (A) Deck is in the foreground. Because of class segregation, there were no stairs connecting these decks. If passengers wanted to continue toward the stern, they had to locate a deck ladder or jump to the decks below. (Olympic)

sense of excitement to many being in the first class area, and having a go at the liquor free of charge. Until now, the room seemed like a good haven from the chaos out on deck. But suddenly the ship began groaning, and the slant of the deck was accelerating so that one could see the tilt worsening before his own eyes. Glasses and bottles and decks of cards and the clock on the fireplace mantle all slid from where they stood and crashed to the floor. There was a terrible rumbling as well, and those in the room realized it was the sound of people running outside on deck toward the stern. Things were falling all around and the same sounds could be heard reverberating throughout the ship. Instantaneously, everyone bolted for the exitways. Many headed for the revolving doors that lead to the palm court at the end of A Deck. Others ran out the forward end of the room to the aft staircase foyer and then out the door onto the Promenade Deck.

As the bow continued to sink, the stern continued to lift out of the water. To those already at the rear of the ship, there was no approaching water to alert them that the Titanic was sinking fast. Standing in the middle of the poop deck, one would have instead noticed that the upper decks in the first and second class areas were suddenly crowding with people arriving from somewhere forward, pressing up against the railings. They seemed to be in a state of panic, and many of them were actually climbing over the railings and jumping down to the lower decks. In the meantime, the deck was slanting more and more by the second. Suddenly, numerous crashes came from the third class general room and smoking room and people came rushing out. But they could only get out so fast, and muffled shouts of panic were heard from within. As steerage passengers streamed out of those rooms, the

This departure scene of the Titanic's sister ship, Olympic illustrates how congested the aft decks of the Titanic must have been as hundreds pressed toward the stern to escape the rising waters.

people on the open decks were squeezed tighter and tighter. Many cried out to others in their families, trying to keep together in the growing chaos.

Those in the third class who elected to remain down on the lower decks to stay warm and away from the crowds were caught off guard when the ship suddenly increased the pace of its forward tilting. A rush from their rooms or corridors to the stairwell was easy enough. In the process, they too heard the crashing of everything that wasn't nailed down sliding forward and falling to the floor. Reaching the third class staircase, however, they were stopped by crowds piled up outside the public rooms. One can only guess how congested this area would have been and the impact it had on anyone still inside the ship.

In the midst of all this were the dogs released from the kennels. Running around the deck, they were as confused as the passengers and crew by the growing tilt of the decks and rush for the stern. Caught up by the movement of the crowd, they may have headed for the stern as well.

The water continued its climb up the boat deck, pouring in through the open door of the gymnasium and submerging the state of the art exercise equipment with an initial splash of foamy seawater. The wave by now was completely spent and the water advanced with a swirling motion. It raced up the promenade deck past the bay windows of the Reading and Writing Room. Quiet as always, and lights still on, the room bore witness as the foamy sea raced by on deck, quickly rising along the outsides of the windows. The advance continued toward the windows of the Main Lounge, as books spilled forward on the elaborate bookshelf, bumping up against the glass casing. Eventually, the rear of the promenade deck, which was not enclosed by windows, dipped below the surface. The ocean poured over the railing and roared down the deck, colliding with the water racing up in the opposite direction.

The angle of the ship was growing now so that it was becoming difficult to stand. As the skylight windows on the boat deck for the Main Lounge slid beneath the water, some of the passengers and crew were still climbing over the deck gates that segregated the first and second class areas from the crew section. With the water lapping at the heels of those in the back of the crowd, panic set in. Some made no headway as the water rose around them. Others pushed their way ahead of other people. Still others headed over to a stairway that lead to the Promenade Deck, ran down the steps, and continued their race toward the stern via A Deck.

It must have been quite imposing to those bottlenecked at the gates near water level to look uphill at the boat deck rising at a 45 degree angle ahead. Items not bolted down on the outside decks, including a number of small iron gates ordinally posted in front of the lifeboats, began sliding down, clanging as they collided with the empty davits along the way. Some tins of water and a few loaves of bread intended for a lifeboat but never loaded came sliding down from somewhere along the deck. Thick wooden masts which had earlier been removed from inside the lifeboats crashed down as well. All of this and more came sliding down the decks into the people. The agile were able to jump or walk over the debris sliding down.

As the stern continued to rise, many must have wondered whether it was such a good idea to be heading there anymore. During the voyage, the boat deck normally rose seventy feet above sea level. Now, they were heading towards the rear of a ship that had risen 250 feet out of the water and was apparently going to stand on end. As the Titanic continued her swan dive, everyone eventually found the deck too difficult to climb. Those who came to a stop without

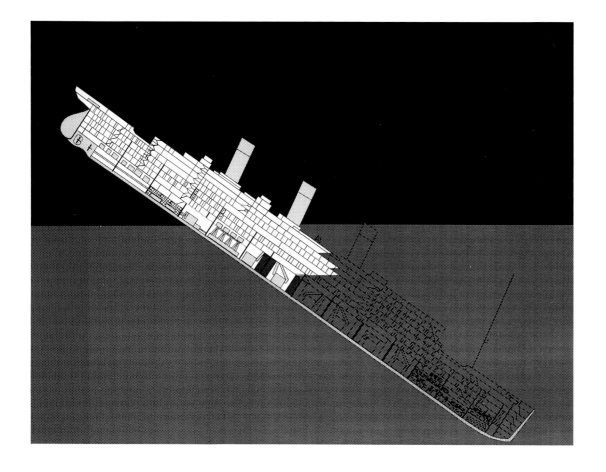

something to hold onto discovered themselves trying to balance on an impossible slant - so they fell.

Everything changed so quickly! So suddenly, in fact, that people had no time to think about what they were doing. One moment, the ship was calmly going down by the bow with a manageable tilt forward. The next minute the ship was in the process of standing on end, throwing everything inside her forward with almost a deafening roar. The gravity of the situation crashed in on everyone now, as the ship tilted forward to a 50 degree slant or more. People began

jumping, especially closer to water line. It was harder for those higher up on the stern. The dark ocean was now far below them, and even under these desperate circumstances it would take a lot of courage to jump over two hundred feet. Most held on.

Many were caught off guard by the sudden turn of events in the ship's condition and did not allow themselves enough time to get out on deck. Several accounts depict passengers and crew indoors until dangerously late in the ship's life. Baker Joughin reported seeing the ship's Doctor O'Loughlin all the way down on E Deck a little before 2:00 A.M. (although Lightoller saw him later near the bridge). Joughin himself was in the pantry on A deck when the plunge began. There were the men in the first class smoking room as well as someone releasing the dogs from the kennels. Then there is Gracie's observation of scores of steerage passengers appearing at the doorway only seconds before the water sealed the exitway off. How many other people were in the ship? How many steerage passengers were in the process of making their way through the ship to find the boat deck? How many of the Titanic's engineers and other crew were still down below in Boiler Room No. 1 and the generator room trying to keep the power on?

Because of the motion an ocean liner typically sees at sea, many items are bolted or nailed in place on board. Included were the Cafe Parisien's wicker tables, the Palm Court's furniture, and the benches out on deck. Those bolted items which were light enough, remained in place with the ship as it went to the bottom of the ocean. But the heavier items began to break loose now and when they did emitted a tremendous roar. Included in this category were the pianos on board, all the ovens and refrigerators in the kitchens, beds, bureaus, mirrors and much more.

Incredibly, the Titanic kept her lights on all this time. Those from the lifeboats watched the Titanic in her final death struggle. What only a moment ago was a graceful ship slipping under quietly, had suddenly become an astonishing sight. This huge, mammoth structure was rising right out of the water into the sky, illuminated with hundreds and hundreds of people clinging to her in complete desperation.

Men swam to collapsible B once more after the funnel fell near it. Some just held on to the side at first while others climbed on top. All of them kept their eyes on the Titanic. Jack Thayer had been sucked below the water when he jumped off the ship and he struggled back to the surface just in time to see the funnel fall. It missed him by twenty or so feet by his estimate, yet the mass of the giant smokestack was enough to cause such a suction that it drew him back under the water. This time, when he came back to the surface, he bumped right up against Collapsible B and grabbed a hold of the side, turning his eyes immediately back to the ship.

Thayer: "Her deck was turned slightly toward us. We could see groups of the almost fifteen hundred people still aboard, clinging in clusters or bunches, like swarming bees; only to fall in masses, pairs or singly, as the great after part of the ship, two hundred and fifty feet of it, rose into the sky, till it reached a sixty-five or seventy degree angle. Here it seemed to pause, and just hung, for what felt like minutes. Gradually she turned her deck away from us, as though to hide from our sight the awful spectacle."

On board, people were huddled all over the ship, holding onto the nearest structure.

Lowe: "She went down by the bow first and inclined at an angle; that is, when she took her final plunge she was inclined at an angle of about 75 degrees."

Abelseth: "... we could see the people were jumping over. There was water coming onto the deck and they were jumping over, then, out in the water."

Those who had been bottle necked by the deck gates that divided the classes were in the area between the third and fourth funnels. As they stood there holding on and watching the water, they heard a very disturbing noise. The deck structures all around them creaked and moaned. The second expansion joint right beneath their feet opened up and everything began cracking and popping.

It was at this moment the Titanic died. She had taken in all the seawater she could stand and had been pulled up to an angle the ship was never designed to handle. Her lights went out, blinked back on for a second, and then went out forever. Up until now, the huge ship illuminated the water around her. Now, everything suddenly went dark. The life and spirit of the Titanic had been extinguished.

Just as the lights went off, the Titanic

experienced a catastrophic failure in her steel structure. It was bad enough that an eleven story ship should be turned on end, but the Titanic was put through much worse. The flooded bow was exerting a downward pressure on the ship. The center of the ship was still buoyant in the water, and was exerting an upward pressure on the ship. The stern, sticking clear out of the water, was exerting a tremendous downward pressure. The Titanic snapped in two.

Alfred Olliver: "I cannot say that I saw it right plain; but to my imagination I did, because the lights went out before she went down. She was well down at the head at first, when we got away from her at first, and to my idea she broke forward, and the afterpart righted itself ..."

Senator Burton: "How far were you away from the boat when she sank?"
Frank Osman: "Sixty to 100 yards. After she got to a certain angle she exploded, broke in halves, and it seemed to me as if all the engines and everything that was in the after part slid out into the forward part ..."
Burton: "What do you think the explosions were?"
Osman: "The boilers bursting."

Burton: "What makes you think that?"
Osman: "The cold water coming under the red-hot boilers caused the explosions."
Burton: "You reasoned that out?"
Osman: "Yes; but you could see the explosions by the smoke coming right up the funnels."
Burton: "Did you see any steam and smoke coming?"
Osman: "Yes"
Burton: "Did you see any sparks?"
Osman: "It was all black, looked like as if it was lumps of coal and all that."
Burton: "Coming up through the funnels?"
Osman: "Through the funnels."
Burton: "Did any water come up?"
Osman: "I never seen no water; only the steam and very black smoke."

Arthur Bright: "She broke in two. All at once she seemed to go up on end, you know, and come down about half way, and then the afterpart righted itself again and the forepart had disappeared."

Those unfortunate enough to be on the ship near the waterline between the third and fourth funnel found themselves in the middle of a structure that was tearing itself apart. They probably never knew what hit

them as the wooden decks, the cables to the smokestack, the glass dome over the aft first class staircase, and the one inch thick steel plates that made up the skin of the ship, all began to literally snap apart within several seconds of each other. The sound was spectacular. As the ship tore apart, the jagged opening on the forward section plunged under the surface, creating an extraordinary suction as water rushed into the huge eleven deck opening. Victims in the immediate area were literally gulped by the inrush of water.

Standing at the last empty lifeboat davit on the starboard side of the boat deck, Abelseth and two family members stood watching.

Abelseth: "I was standing there, and I asked my brother-in-law if he could swim and he said no. I asked my cousin if he could swim and he said no. So we could see the water coming up, the bow of the ship was going down, and there was a kind of an explosion. We could hear the popping and cracking, and the deck raised up and got so steep that the people could not stand on their feet on the deck. So they fell down and slid on the deck into the water right on the ship."

All those who survived that night

The final moments of the Titanic. The ship rears up to an incredible angle - soon halting any further attempts by passengers and crew to reach higher areas. Only seconds after this scene, the ship will tear itself apart between the two visible funnels, casting the Titanic in darkness.

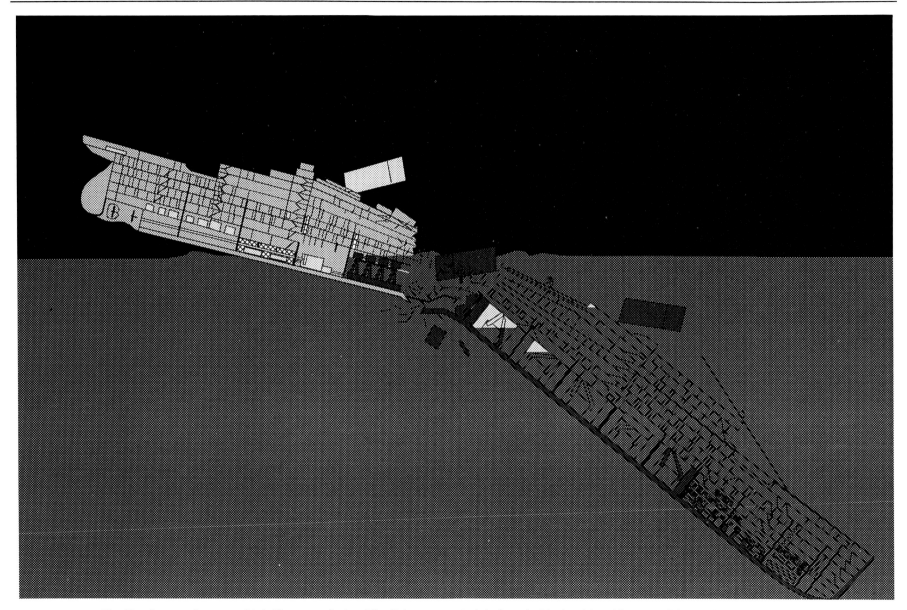

The Titanic snaps in two and it is like an explosion. The lights go out. Debris from inside the ship spills out and descends to the ocean floor.

Was the Titanic's Steel Too Brittle?

Some steel retrieved from the ocean floor at the site of the Titanic disaster revealed an interesting detail about the construction of the liner. Metallurgical tests show that the steel was high in sulphur content, even for steel typically produced in those days. It proved to be brittle.

How did the builder allow brittle steel to be used in the construction of the ship? Tests for steel in 1912 were largely based on hardness. A hard steel was considered a good steel. There were no tests to acknowledge whether a steel was elastic and ductile. The science of metallurgy was slim then, and steel produced was more of an art rather than a science. The principles of tensile strength and elasticity of metals were virtually unknown then. As a result, the steel produced and subsequently accepted by Harland & Wolff was *not* defective by 1912 standards. There was no negligence by the steel manufacturer or shipbuilder based upon the standards of the time. However, this did not help the fact that brittle steel found its way into the Titanic's outer plates.

There is conjecture today that when the Titanic struck the iceberg, the steel plates were too brittle to absorb much of the impact. Submerged in 28 degree water at the time, the steel plates cracked and some even shattered as they rubbed along the ice. If the steel had been more elastic, the plates would have absorbed some of the impact without breaking. Further, critical evidence of the brittleness of the Titanic's steel comes from the actual breakup of the ship. The piece of plating retrieved from the floor was broken, and obviously had come from the area where the ship had torn in two. In examining the steel plate, the metallurgists noted that the break line on the plate was sharp, like broken pottery. Steel with elasticity would have shown some bending around the edge of the plate, indicating that it was absorbing some of the stresses before actually breaking. This steel plate showed no such elasticity.

Naturally, the implication that defective steel, by today's standards, was used in the building of the Titanic created some controversy. In defense of the Titanic's integrity, some have claimed that the steel could not have been that brittle; if it had, it would have broken up long before meeting the iceberg because of the stresses a liner experiences at sea. The ship was certainly capable of withstanding the typical stresses at sea. It just was not capable of surviving a collision with an iceberg.

It is possible that the supply of steel with brittle characteristics was erratic, as evidenced by the Olympic's collision with the HMS Hawke. The Olympic was the sister ship of the Titanic and built alongside her at the same shipyard. One glance at photographs of the damaged Olympic shows that her plates bended quite a bit during the impact. In addition, Titanic samples brought up from the ocean floor in 1996 show some of the steel bended all the way back on itself before breaking. If the elastic properties of the steel fluctuated during construction of the two ships, it is possible that the properties of steel varied within the same ship. One area of the Titanic may have been built with brittle steel, while another area was plated with steel that had better elastic capabilities.

Would the Titanic have escaped disaster if her steel was more ductile? It is certainly possible. Elastic steel is generally a *stronger* steel than an inelastic one, and would have taken the blow from the iceberg better. But the steel plate retrieved for examination was not from the bow so we do not know what elastic properties those plates exhibited when they came in contact with the ice. Finally, it is possible that no amount of elasticity in the steel would have been able to absorb the crushing pressure experienced by the Titanic's bow when her 45,000 tons rubbed along the side of the iceberg.

did so because of one or two key decisions they made, most of them by plain luck instead of thorough forethought. Abelseth was very fortunate that he chose not to jump into the water only a minute earlier. He was lucky that he chose to wait with his cousin and brother-in-law at the empty davits of lifeboat No. 15 - the furthest one back, instead of the davits of lifeboat number 9. Had he chosen either of these alternatives, he would have been caught in the catastrophic breakup of the ship. Because the lights had gone out, he could not see that the ship tore apart a hundred feet ahead of him. He describes the breakup only through the sense of hearing and apparently did not realize himself that he heard the ship tearing in two.

The bow of the ship plunged beneath the water, sucking debris and people down with it and leaving a massive heap of wreckage in its wake. Wood paneling, doors, pieces of railing from the staircase, bureaus, wicker chairs, tables, and clothing, and scores of other debris came floating to the top. Other heavier items were thrown out through the torn openings and plunged with the wreckage to the bottom. Hundreds of miscellaneous items spilled out of the ship including coal from boiler room 1 and cork from the ships lining. The empty davits from lifeboats 9 through 11 were ripped from their mountings as that portion of the boat deck tore apart and dropped toward the ocean floor. The surface became an immediate debris field of everything that could float.

Arthur Peuchen: "... in passing the wreck the next morning I was standing forward, looking to see if I could see any dead bodies, or any of my friends, and to my surprise I saw the barber's pole floating. The barber's pole was on the C deck, my recollection is, the barber shop, and that must have been a tremendous explosion to allow this pole to have broken from its fastenings and drift with the wood."

The water seethed and foamed as huge pockets of air escaped from the submerged bow and burst to the surface. At the same time, volumes of water were being sucked down into the plunging bow. The stern, in the meantime, settled back into the water and righted itself for a moment.

Senator Bourne: "But at no time were you more than 100 yards from the ship from the time you left it?"
Arthur Bright: "Not when she went down."
Bourne: "Did you hear any explosion after you left the ship?"
Bright: "I heard something, but I would not call it an explosion. It was like a rattling of chain, more than anything else."
Bourne: "You did not hear any explosions? You do not think the boilers blew up?"
Bright: "No; it was not like that; it was not such a sound as we would hear if the boilers exploded. It was like a rattling of chain."
Bourne: "The ship went down by her bow first, and you could see the stern and see the keel on the stern, could you?"
Bright: "Yes, sir. Then that righted itself again, got on an even keel again after that."
Bourne: "That is the stern?"
Bright: "It settled down in the water on an even keel."

Many saw this and thought the ship was going to float again. But what they saw was no longer a ship. It was a piece of carcass. Now consisting of the last third of the structure, it sat there for a moment, dark and lifeless with the jagged openings of its decks torn open and fully exposed. A single oil lamp shone brightly on the stern mast as though in religious vigil for the death of the Titanic.

The Ship on the Horizon - Part III
How Far Away Was The Californian?

Although it seems rather obvious that the ship seen on the horizon was the Californian, the subject remains open to discussion to this day because of the nagging inconsistencies in what people saw regarding the movements of both the Titanic and the Californian. One thing is clear, though. The Californian saw the Titanic's distress rockets. Could she have reached the sinking ship in time?

Senator Smith: "If you had received the CQD call of distress from the Titanic Sunday evening after your communication with the Titanic, how long, under the conditions which surrounded you, would it have taken you to have reached the scene of that catastrophe?"
Stanley Lord: "At the very least, two hours."
Smith: "Two hours?"
Lord: "At the very least, the way the ice was packed around us, and it being nighttime."
Smith: "Do you know how long it took for the Carpathia to reach the scene of the accident from the time the CQD call was

received by Captain Rostron?"
Lord: "Only from what I have read in the paper."
Smith: "It took the Carpathia about four hours to reach the scene of the Titanic's accident, after they received word."
Lord: "So I understand."
Smith: "Do you know from your log, or from any other source that you deem accurate, the position of the Carpathia when she received the CQD call?"
Lord: "No, sir."
Smith: "You were about 20 miles away?"
Lord: "Nineteen and one half to twenty miles from the position given me by the Titanic."
Smith: "And the Carpathia was 53 miles away?"
Lord: "Yes, sir."

The Titanic began firing rockets at 12:45 A.M.. This would have given the Californian exactly one hour and thirty five minutes to get to the Titanic if she had responded immediately after seeing the first rocket. Since the Californian was on the

same side of the ice field as the Titanic, she would not have had to work her way out of the ice field for long to reach the Titanic - although it would have been dangerous all the same. The Titanic had miscalculated their position the prior night and because of this error, the Californian headed for the Titanic the following morning toward an incorrect location. As a result, she ended up having to pass through the ice field *twice*.

Smith: "How long did it take you to reach the scene of the accident from the time you steamed up and got under way Monday morning?"
Lord: "I will read from the log book. 'Six o'clock, proceeded slow, pushing through the thick ice. Six twenty, clear of thickest of ice; proceeded full speed, pushing the ice. Eight-thirty, stopped close to steamship Carpathia.'"
Smith: "Was the Carpathia at that time at the scene of the wreck?"
Lord: "Yes sir, she was taking the last of the people out of the boats."

101

This indicates that the Californian took two and a half hours to get to the Carpathia. What Captain Lord does not mention during this part of the questioning is that he had to cross *back* through the ice field a second time to reach the Carpathia. This comes up in passing during another subject later on in the questioning, and the significance does not seem to register with the senators.

Smith: *"Did you see anything of the Frankfurt?"*
Lord: *"Yes."*
Smith: *"Where and when?"*
Lord: *"I met him 5 or 10 minutes past 12, after I was leaving the Titanic, the scene of the disaster. He was running along parallel with the ice, apparently trying to find an opening, and he saw me coming through, and he headed for the place I was coming out, and as we came out he went in. He went through the same place toward the scene of the disaster."*

In addition to passing through the ice field twice, which undoubtedly slowed him down significantly, Captain Rostron observed the Californian approach the lifeboat scene from the *southwest* due to

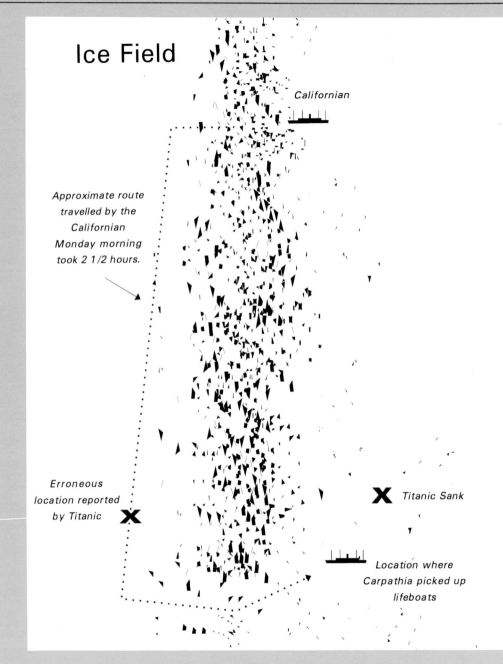

Ice Field

Californian

Approximate route travelled by the Californian Monday morning took 2 1/2 hours.

Erroneous location reported by Titanic

X

X Titanic Sank

Location where Carpathia picked up lifeboats

Lord's search for a break in the ice field to cross through again. This indicates that the Californian traveled south of the Carpathia's position and then turned northeast. In Captain Lord's own words, it took him 2 ½ hours to reach the scene of the disaster - after passing twice through the ice field and overshooting the destination.

During the previous night, the Californian would not have mistakenly traveled through the ice field twice because of the incorrect location reported by the Titanic. Instead, the Californian would have had the luxury of traveling in a straight line towards the lights of the Titanic on the same side of the ice field as she was on. Even taking the icy conditions in the dark under consideration, it becomes obvious that the Californian's travel time would have been significantly shorter than 2 ½ hours.

As a clue to the true distance between the Californian and the Titanic, the lights were clearly visible to the naked eye when viewed from the Titanic's deck, but down near the surface of the water, the lights of the distant ship were difficult to locate.

Senator Fletcher: "After you got in the water did you see the light from this steamer that you had seen previously?"

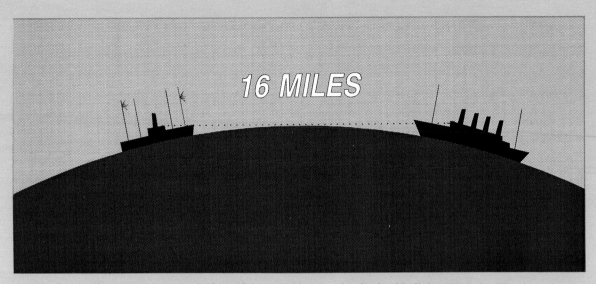

16 MILES

Maximum distance between both ships if they could see each other's side lights. Both the Titanic and Californian witnesses stated they saw the other ship's side lights.

Joseph Boxhall: "Yes. I saw it for a little while and then lost it. When I pulled around the ship I could not see it any more, and did not see it any more."

Eloise Smith: "There was a small light on the horizon that we were told to row toward. Some people seemed to think it was a fishing smack or small boat of some description. However, we seemed to get no nearer the longer we rowed and I am of the opinion it was a star. Many people in our boat said they saw two lights. I could not until I had

looked a long time: I think it was the way our eyes focused and probably the hope for another boat."

Commenting on this evidence at the Senate Hearings was Captain John J. Knapp of the United States Navy Hydrographic Office. Based upon the curvature of the earth, he did an extensive analysis and presented his findings, including the calculated distance of the Californian.

Captain Knapp: "The outer arc around each

ship is drawn with a radius of 16 miles, which is approximately the farthest distance at which the curvature of the earth would have permitted the side lights of the Titanic to be seen by a person at the height of the side lights of the Californian ... The inner circle around each ship is drawn with a radius of 7 miles. This is approximately the distance after reaching which the curvature of the earth would have shut out the side lights of the Californian from the view of one in a lifeboat in the water. It appears, therefore, that if the Titanic's position at the time of the accident was as fixed by the testimony and if it was the side light of the Californian that was seen from the boat deck of the Titanic, the Californian was somewhere inside of the arc of the 16 mile circle drawn about the Titanic. It further appears that if the above hypothesis be correct and if the side light of the other steamer could not be seen, as is testified to, from one of the lifeboats of the Titanic after being lowered, the Californian was somewhere outside of the circle of the 7 mile radius drawn about the Titanic. "

Captain Knapp was saying that the Californian was seven to sixteen miles away from the Titanic. It should be noted that

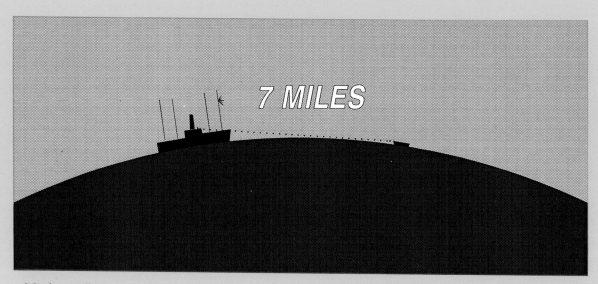

Maximum distance if lifeboats could see the Californian's side lights. Lifeboat survivors apparently did not see the side lights - they only saw the white mast light.

passengers in the lifeboats could just barely see the Californian's *mast* lights which were white and higher than the colored side lights - which they could not see. This would push the distance of the Californian out further away from the seven mile mark. On the other hand, Boxhall had mentioned earlier that when he was on the Titanic's bridge and the Californian presented her side to the Titanic (as she drifted in place), he could clearly see her side lights as though the ship were only four to five miles away. This implies that the Californian's sidelights were more than just

barely visible over the horizon and pulls the estimated distance of the Californian in from the 16 mile maximum.

It is likely that the Californian was much closer than many people think. Most of the estimates of her distance from the Titanic have always heavily relied on the Californian's own stated position, and the amount of time it took for her to reach the scene of the disaster the following morning. But both of these are highly unreliable yardsticks to estimate - particularly since they originate from the very ship who had so much at risk if it was established she could have saved 1,500 lives.

Fitting the pieces above together, she was probably ten miles away - exactly as many on the Titanic had estimated. Captain Smith, with his vast experience, actually told some of the lifeboats to row for the distant ship, unload, and come back. The officer on the Californian's bridge could see an initial burst of light when the distress rocket was ignited, proving he could see the Titanic's bridge even during its sinking state where it would have been lower on the horizon.

So, how long would it have taken the Californian to get to the Titanic ten miles away? Captain Lord, speaking of his ship's readiness on Sunday night when he stopped in the ice field, implied the Californian would not take long to get underway.

Senator Fletcher: "... But you could have gone to the Titanic?"
Lord: "The engines were ready. I gave instructions to the chief engineer, and told him I had decided to stay there all night. I did not think it safe to go ahead. I said, 'We will keep handy in case some of these big fellows come crunching along and get into it.'"

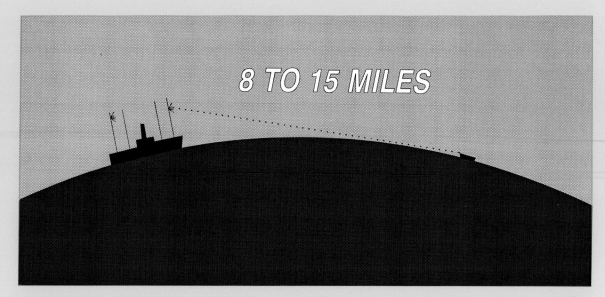

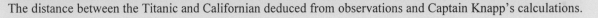

The distance between the Titanic and Californian deduced from observations and Captain Knapp's calculations.

Concerning the Californian' speed ...

Senator Smith: "What is the average speed of the steamship Californian under fair conditions?"
Captain Lord: "On our present consumption we average 11 in fine weather."
Smith: "In case of distress, I suppose it would be possible for you to exceed that considerably."
Lord: "Oh, we made 13 and 13 ½ the day we were going down to the Titanic."

At 13½ knots, it would have taken the Californian 45 minutes to reach the Titanic ten miles away. Again, the first rocket was fired at 12:45A.M. What if the Californian reacted to the first rocket and took 15 minutes before actually getting underway? Because of the ice and the darkness, what if she traveled at a more cautious 10 knots instead of 13½? This would still place the ship at the scene by 2:00 A.M. - in time to assist 1,600 people still trapped on board the sinking Titanic.

Passengers and crew in the water and in the lifeboats watched the stern with great interest now. Many thought it was going to stay afloat in those first few moments. But it was a short lived idea. With all eleven decks ripped open and exposed to the sea, the water rushed in through the broken remains of the stern and it quickly tilted forward again.

Elizabeth Shutes: "A sea, calm as a pond, kept our boat steady, and now that mammoth ship is fast, fast disappearing. Only one tiny light is left - a powerless little spark, a lantern fastened to the mast."

Steerage passengers still on the stern had no idea what had just happened to the ship. All they knew was that the lights went out and the deck leveled enough so they could stand again. Those passengers caught inside found one last chance to get out of the ship and came pouring through the doorways in the dark. The clutter inside the third class general and smoking rooms from fallen furniture and people must have been horrific. The opportunity to get out would be a brief one.

High above the deck the masthead light cast a faint illumination on the scene below. By this point, many on the poop and well decks had no other plan but to wait things out and see what would happen next. And something quickly did. The stern tilted forward until the water reached the boat deck again. There, people still clung to their positions waiting for the right moment to abandon ship.

Abelseth: "Then we hung onto a rope in one of the davits. We were pretty far back at the top deck. My brother-in-law said to me, 'We had better jump off or the suction will take us down.' I said, 'No. We won't jump yet. We ain't got much show anyhow, so we might as well stay as long as we can'. So he stated again, 'We must jump off.' But I said, 'No; not yet'. So, then it was only about 5 feet down to the water when we jumped off. It was not much of a jump."

Meanwhile, down below, the water rushed in through the giant opening and crashed up against the watertight bulkheads. The doors through these bulkheads had been opened at the back of the ship and it is likely they remained open until the end. However, their size was small enough to impede the flow of water compared to the opening created by the breakup. All of the forward deck areas of the stern flooded first, pulling the stern down by the front.

When the water reached the upper decks, there were no watertight bulkheads to hold it back. It roared in through the torn wreckage of the kitchens used for the first and second class dining rooms on D deck. Continuing up that same deck, the water met the second class main staircase and splashed in around the steps. It was the first time all night that the second class area was seeing any water. The ocean raced into the first class accommodations on B and C decks, sweeping up the splintered and broken pieces of the elaborate paneling that lined the hallways. On A deck, it immediately submerged what little was left of the first class lounge and then engulfed the aft first class staircase. By the time the water entered the second class dining room on D deck, the stern had settled back into the water enough to regain some buoyancy. All of this occurred within seconds of the breakup.

The Boat Deck area where Olaus Abelseth and his relatives waited until the water was only a few feet away before jumping. (Olympic)

Although the stern settled back into the water somewhat, it continued its forward slant in the process. Soon the slant forward worsened again and those rooms that were exposed by the tear poured out more of their contents into the water. Pots, pans, plates, heaters, statues, window panes, wine bottles, bathtubs, shoes, combs, and hundreds of other articles spilled out into the water and began their long descent two and a half miles down. Seventy three years later, they would be observed scattered about the ocean floor.

The sea washed in faster on the higher decks than it could get through the watertight doorways of the lower decks. This soon created a top heavy situation and the stern began to roll over on its side. Hundreds of people were still on the decks when the ship rolled over. They slid into the ocean in masses, one on top of the other. The physical abuse of that kind of experience can only be imagined as people crashed down on people, sliding along the teak wooden decks, colliding with benches and cranes and ropes and railings, then finally landing in 28 degree water. By now, only a few people were left on board clinging - or perhaps even stuck to a deck structure. Those still inside the ship would have no further opportunities to escape. Trapped in the darkness of rooms

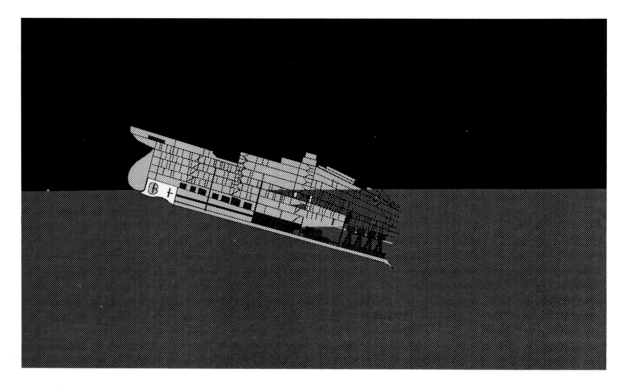

The stern section falls back and rights itself for a moment. But with all its decks opened, it soon sinks.

tipped on their sides, they would go down with the Titanic.

Rosa Abbott was on the open well deck with her two sons, ages nine and fifteen, when the ship rolled over on its side. She held both sons close in her arms as they went over, but amidst the chaos of hundreds falling on top of each other into the icy Atlantic, she lost her grip - and lost them forever. While she was struck by falling people from numerous angles, then hit by pieces of wood rising to the surface from the submerged ship, several of her ribs were broken. Rosa fought for her life and swam away from the crowd, searching for her two children in the chaos all around. Her shouts for her two boys were drowned out by hundreds of other cries.

The broken stern section rolls on its side, dumping scores of victims into the icy waters.

The mast head light went under water, plunging the scene into total darkness. Now, only the black outline of the stern stood out against the starlit sky. Baker Joughin was along the starboard rail of the well deck when the stern rolled over. Holding onto the railing, he climbed over when the angle presented itself and literally stood on the side of what was left of the ship. The broken piece of stern was submerged at the front as well as lying on its side. Slowly, it began to stand up on end again. As it did, Baker Joughin nimbly walked along its side up around the curve of the outer edge to the very back of the stern.

Hissing, gurgling and rumbling like some kind of medieval dragon, the stern rose up on end again, but not nearly as high as a couple of minutes earlier. Finally, it stood straight up into the air. It reminded one passenger of a finger pointing up to the sky. With so much air trapped inside and only the open portholes to let it escape, the stern began to slip under very, very slowly.

Hugh Woolner: "She seemed to me to stop for about 30 seconds at one place before she took the final plunge, because I watched one particular porthole, and the water did not rise there for at least half a minute, and then she suddenly slid under with her propellers under the water."

Henry Etches: "She seemed to raise once as though she was going to take a violent dive, but sort of checked, as though she had scooped the water up and had leveled herself. She then seemed to settle very, very quiet, until the last, when she rose up and she seemed to stand twenty seconds, stern in that position (indicating) and then she went down with an awful grating, like a small boat running off a shingly beach."

No doubt the grating noise that Etches heard was the sound of air under pressure rushing out of every opening of the ship.

Thayer: "We had an oar on our overturned boat. In spite of several men working it, amid our cries and prayers, we were being gradually sucked in toward the great pivoting mass. I looked upwards - we were right underneath the three enormous propellers. For an instant, I thought they were sure to come right down on top of us. Then, with the deadened noise of the bursting of her last few gallant bulkheads, she slid quietly away from us into the sea."

Over 2,000 people watched as it began its final descent. It went down very slowly - to many it seemed like an eternity. Some thought it was 30 seconds, others thought it was more like five minutes. With a continuous hissing, it slid under an inch at a time. And then it was gone. The Titanic had sunk.

Bride: "When at last the waves washed over her rudder there wasn't the least bit of suction I could feel. She must have kept going just so slowly as she had been."

The disappearance of the stern was almost anticlimactic compared to the Titanic's behavior over the past several minutes. It did not go down with a great suction or wave. Instead, it went under with a whisper, slower than a descending elevator coming to a stop. Baker Joughin was standing on the stern when it went under and did not even get his hair wet. No sooner did Joughin step off the side of the ship than he came across the same overturned boat that Lightoller and Thayer were on.

Joughin: "I do not believe my head went under the water at all. I thought I saw some wreckage. Swam towards it and found collapsible boat B with Lightoller and about twenty-five men on it. There was no room for me. I tried to get on, but was pushed off, but I hung around. I got around to the opposite side and cook Maynard, who recognized me, helped me and held onto me."

1,500 people were now in the water with their senses virtually knocked out of them. The Titanic was gone and they were up to their shoulders in the dark icy Atlantic under a starlit night. Many were hurt from falling off the ship. Lifeboat number 4 was so close to the scene of the disaster that it picked up five more people shortly after the sinking before rowing away.

Mrs. Stephenson: "When the call came that she was going I covered my face and heard some one call, 'She's broken'. After what seemed a long time I turned my head only to see the stern almost perpendicular in the air so that the full outline of the blades of the propeller showed above the water. She then gave her final plunge and the air was filled with cries. We rowed back and pulled in five more men from the sea. Their suffering from the icy water was intense and two men who had been pulled into the stern afterwards died ..."

But lifeboat number 4 did not even scratch the surface in regards to the number of people floating about.

Gracie: "What impressed me at the time that my eyes beheld the horrible scene was a thin light-gray smoky vapor that hung like a pall a few feet above the broad expanse of sea that was covered with a mass of tangled wreckage. That it was a tangible vapor, and not a product of imagination, I feel well assured. It may have been caused by smoke or steam rising to the surface around the area where the ship had sunk. At any rate it produced a supernatural effect, and the pictures I had seen by Dante and the description I had read in my Virgil of the infernal regions of Charon, and the River Lethe, were then uppermost in my thoughts. Add to this, within the area described, which was as far as my eyes could reach, there arose to the sky the most horrible sounds ever heard by mortal man except by those of us who survived this terrible tragedy. The agonizing cries of death from over a thousand throats, the wails and groans of the suffering, the shrieks of the terror-stricken and the awful gaspings for breath of those in the last throes of drowning, none of us will ever forget to our dying day."

Gracie at first clung to a plank and a crate but was lucky enough to soon wander across collapsible B, still upside down. He climbed on its back before it became so overcrowded that others were fought back with oars and pieces of wood.

In the meantime, hundreds and hundreds of others floated about. The water was so icy cold that once they managed to get their breaths back, they began to panic. They knew there were lifeboats out there and they began to scream for help. They began to scream for other members of their families who were separated when the stern rolled over onto its side. Many just screamed from the painful cold of the water. Within minutes they were all crying out and the sounds carried across the water that night to the lifeboats.

George Harder: "After it went down, we heard a lot of these cries and yells. You could not hear any shouts for help or anything like that. It was a sort of continuous yelling or moaning."

Eloise Smith: "The cries we heard I thought were seamen, or possibly steerage who had overslept, it not occurring to me for a moment that my husband and my friends were not saved."

Frederick Clench: "There were awful cries, and yelling and shouting and that. Of course, I told the women in the boats to remain quiet and consoled them a bit. I told them it was men in the boats shouting out to the others, to keep them from getting away from one another."

As time went by, many in the water found their friends and families in the wreckage and swam to them. Some formed circles by locking their arms together. It must have been some comfort to those who found the people that mattered to them most. Floating in that icy water for the first few minutes, they may have thought it possible to wait together until help came. Some probably looked for the light on the horizon or any sign that the mysterious ship was approaching. Others swam around as the adrenaline in their systems forced them to struggle for life.

Bride: "I felt, after a little while, like sinking. I was very cold. I saw a boat of some kind near me and put all my strength into an effort to swim to it. It was hard work. I was all done when a hand reached out from the boat

Overturned collapsible B is found still floating upside down a week after the disaster. This was the lifeboat that Bride climbed aboard to get out of the icy water.

and pulled me aboard. It was our same collapsible. The same crowd on it. There was just room for me to roll on the edge. I lay there, not caring what happened. Somebody sat on my legs. They were wedged in between slats and were being wrenched. I had not the heart left to ask the man to move. It was a

terrible sight all around - men swimming and sinking."

Bride climbed once again aboard the overturned collapsible B. His destiny seemed linked to that boat.

Abelseth: "My brother-in-law took my hand just as we jumped off, and my cousin jumped at the same time. When we came into the water, I think it was from the suction, or anyway we went under, and I swallowed some water. I got a rope tangled around me, and I let loose of my brother-in-law's hand to get away from the rope. I thought then, 'I am a goner'. That is what I thought when I got tangled up in this rope. But I came on top again, and I was trying to swim, and there was a man - lots of them were floating around - and he got me on the neck like that and pressed me under, trying to get on top of me. I said to him, 'Let go!' Of course, he did not pay any attention to that, but I got away from him. Then there was another man and he hung on to me for a while, but he let go. Then I swam; I could not say, but it must have been about 15 or 20 minutes. It could not have been over that. Then I saw something dark ahead of me. I did not know what it was, but I swam toward that, and it was one of those collapsible boats."

Abelseth wandered upon collapsible A, which was still upright but completely swamped with water. The canvas sides were never erected and were level with the sea. This boat bobbed around the sinking liner just about the entire time the Titanic plunged under. It is incredible that it did not get sucked down with the bow when the ship tore in two. To highlight the randomness of events within the wreckage, only a dozen or so people climbed aboard this collapsible. In contrast, overturned collapsible B had so many people on it that others in the water were eventually forced away. With so many suffering and flailing, collapsible A, with only a dozen or so occupants, floated about the wreckage like some type of odd secret club.

Abelseth: "When I got on this raft or collapsible boat, they did not try to push me off, and they did not do anything for me to get on. All they said when I got on there was, 'Don't capsize the boat.' So I hung onto the raft for a little while before I got on. Some of them were trying to get up on their feet. They were sitting down or lying down on the raft. Some of them fell into the water again. Some of them were frozen; and there were two dead that they threw overboard. I got on this raft or collapsible boat and raised up, and then I was continually moving my arms and swinging them around to keep warm. There was one lady aboard this raft, and she got saved. There were also two Swedes, and a first class passenger, I believe that is what he said, and he had just his underwear on. I asked him if he was married, and he said he had a wife and a child. There was also a fireman named Thompson on the same raft. He had burned one of his hands. Also there was a young boy, with a name that sounded like Volunteer."

Standing nearby Abelseth was Rosa Abbott, determined to survive. Bruised and battered and with broken ribs, she stayed on her feet with the others to avoid the deadly cold water. Those that tired and sat down eventually froze from the water in the boat and fell off.

The screams continued from those still drifting about. The water was so cold that their arms and legs ached. Most shivered uncontrollably for a while, then started to feel numb. Exhaustion from the cold was setting in and it was getting harder to cry out. Surely, a boat would come soon to take them out of the water.

With the exception of lifeboat number 4, which had not gotten far from the ship by the time it sank, Fifth Officer Lowe in number 14 was the only other person who returned with the intent to pick up survivors. In the rest of the lifeboats, there was an overwhelming objection to anybody who even suggested going back. Even Lowe decided it would be suicide to go back into the middle of the scene right away, and decided to wait a while first.

Smith: *"You lay off a bit until the drowning people had quieted down?"*
Lowe: *"Yes."*
Smith: *"Then you went to the scene of the wreck?"*
Lowe: *"Yes."*
Smith: *"Had their cries quieted down before you started?"*
Lowe: *"Yes; they had subsided a good deal. It would not have been wise or safe for me to have gone there before, because the whole lot of us would have been swamped and then nobody would have been saved."*
Smith: *"But your boat had, according to your own admission, a water capacity of 65 people?"*
Lowe: *"Yes, but then what are you going to do with a boat of 65 where 1,600 people are drowning?"*
Smith: *"You could have saved 15."*
Lowe: *"You could not do it sir."*
Smith: *"At least, you made no attempt to do it?"*
Lowe: *" I made the attempt sir, as soon as*

any man could do so, and I am not scared of saying it. I did not hang back or anything else."*
Smith: *"I am not saying you hung back. I am just saying that you said you lay by until it had quieted down."*
Lowe: *"You had to do so. It was absolutely not safe. You could not do otherwise because you would have hundreds of people around your boat, and the boat would go down just like that."*
Smith: *"About how long did you lay by?"*
Lowe: *"I should say an hour and a half; somewhere under two hours."*

Finally, Lowe decided it was safe to return to the scene of the sinking and pick up survivors. Had he been in the water himself, he probably would not have waited so long, but since he stepped off the Titanic directly into lifeboat number 15, he did not realize how deadly the water actually was. To his credit, he at least did return. No other lifeboats had the courage.

Lowe: *"Then I went off and I rowed off to the wreckage and around the wreckage and I picked up four people. But one died, and that was a Mr. Hoyt, of New York, and it took all the boat's crew to pull this gentleman into*

the boat, because he was an enormous man, and I suppose he had been soaked fairly well with water, and when we picked him up he was bleeding from the mouth and from the nose. So we did get him on board and I propped him up at the stern of the boat, and we let go his collar, took his collar off, and loosened his shirt so as to give him every chance to breathe; but unfortunately, he died. I suppose he was too far gone when we picked him up. But the other three survived. I then left the wreck. I went right around and strange to say, I did not see a single female body, not one, around the wreckage."*

The description of Mr. Hoyt's condition serves to highlight the physical bruising many of the passengers must have taken when the ship stood on end and dumped them into the water on top of one another.

Charlotte Collyer: *"A little further on we saw a floating door that must have been torn loose when the ship went down. Lying upon it, face downward, was a small Japanese. He had lashed himself with a rope to his frail raft, using the broken hinges to make the knots secure. As far as we could see, he was dead. The sea washed over him every time the door bobbed up and down, and he was frozen stiff. He did not answer when he was hailed, and the officer hesitated about trying to save him. 'What's the use?', said Mr. Lowe. 'He's dead, likely, and if he isn't there's others better worth saving than a Jap!' He had actually turned our boat around, but he changed his mind and went back. The Japanese was hauled on board, and one of the women rubbed his chest, while others chafed his hands and feet. In less time than it takes to tell, he opened his eyes. He spoke to us in his own tongue; then seeing that we did not understand, he struggled to his feet, stretched his arms above his head, stamped his feet and in five minutes or so had almost recovered his strength. One of the sailors near to him was so tired that he could hardly pull his oar. The Japanese bustled over, pushed him from his seat, took his oar and worked like a hero until we were finally picked up. I saw Mr. Lowe watching him in open mouthed surprise. 'By jove!' muttered the officer, 'I'm ashamed of what I said about the little blighter. I'd save the likes o' him six times over if I got the chance.'"*

When Lowe pulled a fourth person out of the water, he unknowingly rescued the very last survivor of the Titanic disaster.

For the remaining 1,500 people in the water, help would never come. Even though their life jackets kept their heads above water, their bodies went numb. As eighteen lifeboats stood nearby with seats for 500 more passengers, the cries for help began to taper off. Drifting in the dark, a quiet took over the scene. Nobody had the strength to yell anymore as the cold drained away any remaining energy. Some talked to each other to try and keep their spirits up. But soon it was too hard to even speak. Quietly they floated in the darkness as a sleepiness began to overtake them. Those in groups took little notice of each other after a while. One by one they lost consciousness. Then, one by one, they died.

Beesley: "The cries, which were loud and numerous at first, died away gradually one by one, but the night was clear, frosty and still, the water smooth, and the sounds must have carried on its level surface free from any obstruction for miles, certainly much farther from the ship than we were situated. I think the last of them must have been heard nearly forty minutes after the Titanic sank. Lifebelts would keep the survivors afloat for hours; but the cold water was what stopped the cries."

The lifeboats drifted about in the dark for hours. Although arguments had broken out on several of the lifeboats earlier, they all eventually settled into a quiet wait, listening to the small ripples of the sea bump up against the sides of their boat. The night was brilliant with stars, and occasionally one would shoot across the sky. How strange everything must have been during those hours. The past events must have seemed unreal. After all, they had just watched the largest ship in the world stand on end and plunge beneath the ocean. It seemed like only minutes ago they were tucked away in their warm beds with the hum of the ship's engines in the background. Now they were bobbing about in a lifeboat in the Atlantic ocean. Sitting there in total darkness, it was almost as if the Titanic never existed - as though it had all been some dream.

Joseph Boxhall: "A little while after the ship's lights went out and the cries subsided, then I found out that we were near the ice. I heard the water rumbling or breaking on the ice. Then I knew that there was a lot of ice about, but I could not see it from the boat."

Some of the lifeboats rowed for the light of the mysterious ship on the horizon all night. Others just sat in the boats and drifted with the currents. For those on collapsibles A and B, time went by in a torturously slow way. Collapsible A was so swamped that the occupants stood in freezing water up to their knees the rest of the night.

Abelseth: "There was one man from New Jersey that I came in company with from London. I do not know what his name was. I tried to keep this man alive; but I could not make it. It was just at the break of day, and he was lying down, and he seemed to be kind of unconscious; he was not really dead, and I took him by the shoulder and raised him up so that he was sitting up on this deck. I said to him, 'We can see a ship now. Brace up.' And I took one of his hands and raised it up like that, and I took him by the shoulder and shook him and he said, 'Who are you?' He said, 'Let me be. Who are you?' I held him up like that for a while but I got tired and cold, and I took a little piece of a small board, a lot of which were floating around there, and laid it under his head on the edge of the boat to keep his head from the water; but it was not more than about half an hour or so when he died."

The occupants of collapsibles A and

Tired and cold, the occupants of collapsible D approach the Carpathia in the early morning hours. The boat contains Woolner, Steffanson, Hoyt, and Mrs. Brown among others. Edith Evans is not one of the occupants.

B yelled for help, but for hours nobody came to their rescue. The air under B slowly leaked out and the underside was awash. Bride's leg was pinned under another body for hours until he could not stand up even if he wanted to. His feet were frostbitten by the cold and lack of circulation. As he sat in the wash, most stood and leaned in various directions to prevent the collapsible from tipping them all into the water.

Gracie: "The suffering on the boat from cold

was intense. My neighbor in front, whom I had pulled aboard, must also have been suffering from exhaustion, but it was astern of us whence came later the reports about fellow boat mates who gave up the struggle and fell off from exhaustion, or died, unable to stand the exposure and strain."

Some time after his disastrously late return to the scene of the sinking, Lowe wandered across the pathetic collapsible A.

Frederick Crowe: "We stopped until daybreak, and we saw in the distance an Engelhardt collapsible boat with a crew of men in it. We went over to the boat and found twenty men and one woman; also three dead bodies, which we left."

He transferred the survivors, who included Abelseth, Williams, a tournament tennis player, Rheims, Daly, and Abbott. Abbott was so physically battered from her experience at the stern of the Titanic that she would not be moved from the infirmary of the rescue ship all the way to New York, and even then would be rushed to the hospital where she would spend another two weeks.

Eventually, lifeboats 12 and 4 found collapsible B at daybreak and took all 30 or

so survivors off, including Gracie, Lightoller, Thayer, Joughin, Bride, and Collins.

Mrs. Stephenson: "... cries of 'Ship Ahoy' and a long low moan came to us and an officer in command of one of the boats ordered us to follow him. We felt that we were already too crowded to go, but our men, with quartermaster and boatswain in command, followed the officer and we pulled over to what proved to be an overturned boat crowded with men. We had to approach it very cautiously, fearing our wash would sweep them off. We could take only a few and they had to come very cautiously. The other boat (No. 12) took most of them and we then rowed away."

As the first hint of light appeared on the eastern horizon, so too did the rescue ship Carpathia. One of the lifeboats lit a flare which was extremely helpful to Captain Rostron on the Carpathia; he was able to turn his ship straight for the boats. However, he did not want to risk running them over in the darkness so he stopped nearby the first boat he reached and did not move again until the rescue was completed. One by one they approached the ship. Some of them had to row several miles to get to it, but eventually

they all made it and were pulled in. Just as the last survivors were climbing on board, the Californian arrived, having heard the news at daybreak when their wireless operator had been awakened and turned on his set.

When the sun came up, about a dozen icebergs could be seen in the area along with a vast ice field to the west that stretched as far as the eye could see. One ominous iceberg in particular floated off in the distance. With a red smear of paint at its waterline, the morning sun glistened on its peak, sending a reflection of light into the eyes of the survivors and crew gazing out over the railing of the rescue ship. It was a wake-up call with a timeless message.

Survivors and Others

The survivors quoted in this book came from all areas of the ship in an attempt to round out the impressions of the disaster. Most accounts were extracted from the Senate transcripts. A few came from articles and books. The following is a very brief biography of those whose accounts were used in this book:

Abelseth, Olaus - a third class passenger who went down with the ship, but survived by climbing aboard a swamped lifeboat.

Beesley, Lawrence - second class passenger who escaped in lifeboat number 13.

Boxhall, Joseph - fourth officer left in lifeboat 2.

Bourne, Senator Jonathan - assisted Senator Smith with the Titanic hearings in Washington.

Bride, Harold - junior wireless operator went down with the ship but survived by clinging to an overturned raft in the wreckage.

Bright, Arthur - Quartermaster on the ship.

Burton, Senator Theodore - assisted Senator Smith with the Titanic hearings in Washington.

Clench, Frederick - seaman who helped man lifeboat number 12.

Collins, John - assistant cook for the first class dining room. who went down with the ship but survived by climbing onto an overturned lifeboat.

Collyer, Charlotte - third class passenger who escaped in a lifeboat.

Crawford, Alfred - first class bedroom steward who helped man lifeboat 8.

Crowe, Frederick - dining room steward who escaped in lifeboat 14.

Daly, Eugene - third class passenger who went down with the ship but survived by climbing onto a swamped lifeboat in the wreckage.

Etches, Henry - first class bedroom steward who helped man lifeboat 5.

Fleet, Frederick - was in the lookouts nest when the ship collided with the iceberg.

Fletcher, Senator Duncan - assisted Senator Smith with the Titanic hearings in Washington.

Goldsmith, Frankie - a third class boy traveling with his mother and father.

Gracie, Archibald - first class passenger who went down with the ship but survived by climbing on top of an overturned lifeboat.

Gill, Ernest - seaman on the steamer Californian who saw rockets fired on the horizon.

Harder, George - first class passenger who escaped in lifeboat 5.

Hardy, John - chief steward for second class who escaped in collapsible D.

Hemming, Samuel - lamptrimmer. Kept lamps lit aboard the ship. Placed lanterns into lifeboats.

Hoyt, Frederick - first class passenger picked up by collapsible D just after jumping into the water.

Ismay, Bruce - managing director of the White Star Line. He was on board to see how the Titanic performed on her maiden voyage.

Jansen, Carl - third class passenger who went down with the ship but survived by climbing aboard an overturned lifeboat. Misidentified as Carl "Johnson" in a New York Times article.

Joughin, Joseph - baker who went down with the ship but survived by climbing aboard an overturned lifeboat in the wreckage.

Knapp, John - captain in the U.S. Navy Hydrographic office who testified on the likely distance the Californian was from the Titanic.

Lightoller, Charles - second officer of the Titanic. The only senior officer to survive.

Lord, Stanley - captain of the steamer Californian nearby the Titanic during the sinking.

Lowe, Harold - fifth officer of the Titanic who manned lifeboat 14.

Newlands, Francis - U.S. Senator who assisted with the Titanic hearings.

Olliver, Alfred - crewman. Quartermaster.

Osman, Frank - seaman who helped man lifeboat 2.

Peuchen, Arthur - first class passenger who escaped in lifeboat 4.

Pitman, Herbert - third officer of the Titanic who helped man lifeboat number 5.

Rheims, George - first class passenger who went down with the ship but survived by climbing onto a swamped lifeboat floating in the wreckage.

Rowe, George - crewman on the ship. Quartermaster.

Ryerson, Emily - first class passenger who escaped in lifeboat number 4.

Shutes, Elizabeth - first class passenger who escaped in a lifeboat.

Smith, Eloise - first class passenger who escaped in lifeboat number 6.

Smith, William - senator for the U.S. who headed up the hearings on the Titanic disaster only days after the sinking.

Stengel, Henry - first class passenger who escaped in lifeboat number 1.

Stephenson, Mrs. - first class passenger who escaped in lifeboat number 4.

Stone, Herbert - second officer on the steamer Californian who watched the Titanic on the distant horizon fire distress rockets.

Taylor, W. - fireman who escaped in lifeboat 15.

Thayer, Jack - teenager traveling first class with his parents.

Ward, William - dining room steward for second class who helped man lifeboat 9.

Weikman, A. - second class barber who went down with ship, survived by climbing onto deck chairs.

White, J. Stuart - first class passenger who escaped in lifeboat number 8.

Woolner, Hugh - first class passenger who survived by leaping into the last lifeboat as it descended.

Glossary

The language of the sea has its own unique words. The following are some used in this book.

Aft - toward the rear, in the direction of the stern of the ship.

Boat Deck - the top deck of the ship that contained all of the lifeboats.

Boiler Rooms - four stories high containing furnaces, or "boilers" to burn coal creating heat to generate steam to drive the engines. There were six boiler rooms along the middle section of the bottom of the ship.

Bow - the front of the ship.

Bridge - area at the very front of the boat deck where the ship was navigated. Although the room in the center is the main part of the bridge, the open deck immediately on both sides is also considered part of the bridge.

Bulkhead - wall.

Cabin - room.

Classes - the Titanic had three; first, second, and third class. First class was the most comfortable way to travel, second was standard, and third was economy. During routine travel, third class was not allowed into the second class areas, and second and third class were not allowed into first class.

Collapsible - a lifeboat with canvas sides which would lift up into place. There were four on the ship and two were successfully launched. The other two floated off the ship as it went under.

Davits - The steel "arms" that held the ropes and lifeboats over the side of the ship while it was being lowered.

Decks - floors. On the Titanic, the boat deck was the highest, followed by A, B, C, D, E, and F decks. There were four more decks below F deck at the bow and the stern. The boiler rooms in the middle were four decks high.

Docking Bridge - The small enclosed area on opposite sides of the bridge at the forward corners of the boat deck.

Falls - the mechanisms and ropes used to lower each lifeboat. There were two per lifeboat, the forward falls and the afterfalls.

Forecastle Deck - the open deck at the very front of the ship.

Founder - to sink.

Funnel - smokestack. The Titanic had four, the fourth being a dummy and used only for ventilation and steam exhaust.

Gangway Doors - doors located on the sides of the ship at various locations on different decks.

Grand Staircase - an elaborate staircase that ran all the way from boat deck down to E deck in the first class area. It was one of the showpieces of the Titanic.

Gunwale - the upper edge of a ship's side.

Knots- a measurement of distance. One knot equals 1.15 mile. The Titanic's approximate speed of 22 knots would equate to 25 miles per hour.

Lifebelt- same as life preserver and life vest. They were made of white canvas with cork slabs sewn inside them and were fastened around the upper sides of a person.

List - tilt, slant.

Masts - poles. The Titanic had two; one was a foremast near the bow and the other a stern mast.

Passageways- corridors and/or entranceways on a ship.

Poop Deck - the open deck at the very back of the ship.

Port - when standing on the ship facing forward, the left side.

Promenade Deck - one deck below the boat deck, it was another name for A deck because it had a promenade walkway the full length of the deck on both sides of the ship.

Running Lights - located on the outside of the ship on both sides, they were an indication to a distant ship of which direction a vessel was pointing. A green light was on the starboard side, and a red on the port.

Service Speed - the standard and economical speed at which a ship would routinely travel at while in service.

Scotland Road - another name for the E deck corridor on the port side of that deck that virtually ran the entire length of the ship from bow to stern.

Sidelights - same as running lights.

Starboard - the right side of the ship.

Steerage Passengers - same as third class passengers.

Stern - the back of the ship.

Watertight Compartments - divisions created by watertight bulkheads throughout the bottom of the ship. Unfortunately for the Titanic, they were not sealed off at the top, being open by stairs.

Well Deck - there were two of them. They were the open deck areas just forward of the poop deck at the stern, and just behind the forecastle deck at the bow.

Wireless - the early use of radio. Voice could not be transmitted, but instead a series of short signals representing letters of the alphabet would be transmitted to send messages.

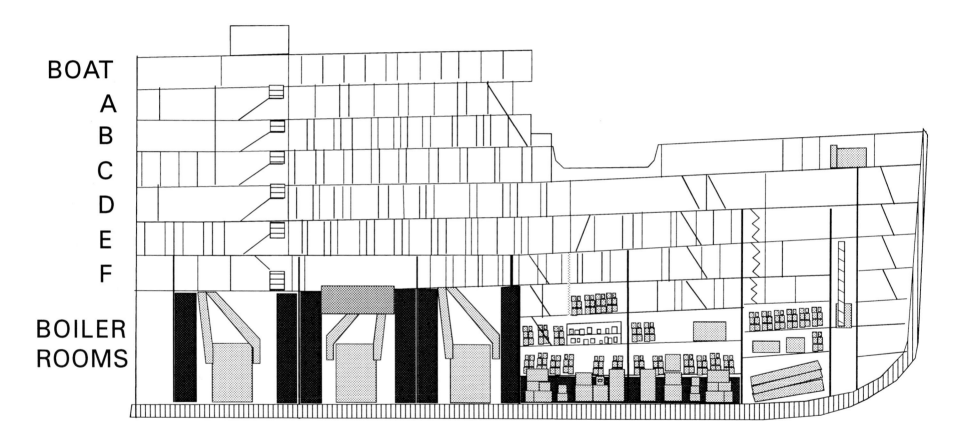

BOAT
A
B
C
D
E
F

BOILER
ROOMS

Bibliography

Ballard, Robert D. *The Discovery of the Titanic.* New York: Warner Books, 1987.

Ballard, Robert D. *Exploring the Titanic.* Toronto: Madison Press, 1988.

Beesley, Lawrence. *The Loss of the Titanic.* London: William Heinemann, 1912.

Bride, Harold. *Thrilling Tale by Titanic's Wireless Man.* New York: New York Times, 1912.

Bonsall, Thomas E. *Titanic.* New York: Gallery Books, 1987.

Davie, Michael. *Titanic, The Death and Life of a Legend.* New York: Alfred A. Knopf, 1987.

Eaton, John P. & Haas, Charles A. *Titanic, Triumph and Traged.* New York: Norton, 1986.

Eaton, John P. & Haas, Charles A. *Titanic, Destination Disaster.* New York: Norton, 1987.

Goldsmith, Frank J. *Echoes in the Night.* Indian Orchard: Titanic Historical Society, 1991.

Gracie, Archibald. *The Truth About the Titanic.* New York: Mitchell Kennerley, 1913.

Kamuda, Edward. *The Passing of Time and Memories.* Indian Orchard: THS, 1995.

Lightoller, Charles H. *Titanic and Other Ships.* London: Ivor Nicholson and Watson, 1935.

Lord, Walter. *A Night to Remember.* New York: Henry Holt & Company, 1955.

Lord, Walter. *The Night Lives On.* New York: William Morrow and Company, Inc., 1986.

Lynch, Don & Marschall, Ken. *Titanic, An Illustrated History.* New York: Madison Press, 1992.

Marcus, Geoffrey. *The Maiden Voyage.* London: George Allen and Unwin, 1969.

Miller, William. *The First Great Ocean Liners.* Mineola: Dover, 1984.

Mills, Simon. *Olympic, The Old Reliable.* Dorset: Waterfront Publications, 1993.

Mowbray, Jay. *The Sinking of the Titanic.* Harrisburg: Mintor Company, 1912.

Myers, L.T. *The Sinking of the Titanic and Great Sea Disasters.* 1912.

Pellegrino, Charles. *Her Name, Titanic.* New York: Avon, 1988.

Rostron, Arthur H. *Home From the Sea.* New York: Macmillan Company, 1931.

Shaum, John & Flayhart, William. *Majesty at Sea.* New York: Norton, 1981.

Titanic Commutator. Indian Orchard: Titanic Historical Society, Quarterly.

U.S. Senate. *Titanic Disaster Hearings.* Washington: Government Printing Office, 1912.

Wade, Wyn Craig. *The Titanic: End of a Dream.* New York: Rawson Wade Publishers, 1979.

White, Alma. *The Titanic Tragedy, God Speaking to the Nations.* Bound Brooks, 1912.

Winocour, Jack. *The Story of the Titanic as Told by it's Survivors.* New York: Dover, 1960.

Acknowledgments

I would like to express my thanks first to the Titanic Historical Society for enabling a focus on this timeless subject. In addition to the invaluable source of accurate information that they are, the society has served as a conduit for a wealth of talent that has kept this subject alive for 85 years. Special thanks to Ed and Karen Kamuda for their perspective in general on the subject, and particularly Ed's wisdom on the accuracy of survivor accounts with the passing of time. Thanks to Don Lynch for the information on some of the Titanic's officers.

My gratitude extends to Lisa Jesmain for her input and perspective on the social attitudes of the period and the numerous discussions I had with her on virtually every aspect of the Titanic. Those conversations, as well as the encouraging words received after each completed painting kept me motivated to continue the project through several tough times.

Additional thanks to Tom McCluskie of Harland & Wolff for his position on the integrity of the steel used in the construction of the Titanic.

Much appreciation is extended to Father Roberto Pirrone whose breathtaking cutaway model is on display at the Los Angeles Maritime Museum. The model immediately drove home the reality of a vast network of corridors and rooms in the Titanic, making it clear what the third class passengers were up against as they struggled to find their way to the boat deck.

Thanks as well to my father. His tireless search for used books on ocean liners brought to my fingertips a wealth of information.

And finally, most of my thanks to my wife for her excellent ideas on the paintings and text while they were a work in progress. Thanks for maintaining some sense of sanity in a household with two preschoolers and a man obsessed with painting scenes of the Titanic.

Index

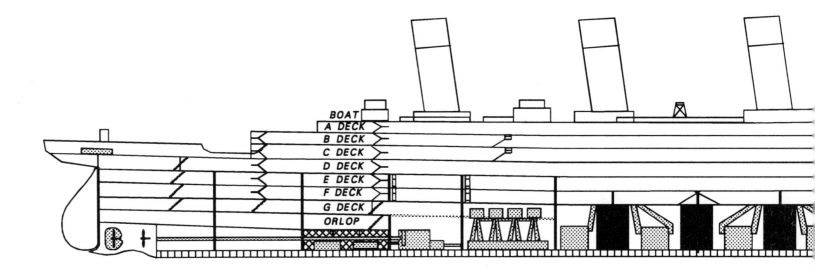

BOAT
A DECK
B DECK
C DECK
D DECK
E DECK
F DECK
G DECK
ORLOP